T0392908

Understanding Emotions in English Language Learning in Virtual Worlds

This book contributes to overcoming the deficit in research on emotions in foreign language learning in the domain of computer-assisted language learning (CALL) in both traditional and virtual settings.

The authors divide emotions into positive (i.e., enjoyment and curiosity) and negative (i.e., boredom and language anxiety) and explore their role in L2 teaching and learning in CALL environments from theoretical, empirical and pedagogical perspectives. The book begins with a theoretical overview of selected issues concerning positive and negative emotions and surveys the studies that have dealt with this issue in L2 learning in conventional settings and CALL. The empirical part of the book is devoted to a research project which explores the experience of positive and negative emotions in learning English in the virtual world Second Life, the relationships of the emotions in question and factors influencing them. The book concludes by recommending a selection of practices which can help maximize the positive emotions and minimize the negative emotions in foreign language learning in CALL environments.

This is an important and illuminating read for students and scholars of applied linguistics, second language education and educational technology who are interested in CALL and in incorporating VW/VR-based language learning programs into their studies and teaching.

Mariusz Kruk, PhD, works at the University of Zielona Góra, Poland. His main areas of interest include individual difference variables (e.g., boredom, motivation, anxiety) and the application of technology in foreign language learning and teaching.

Mirosław Pawlak is Professor of English at Adam Mickiewicz University, Kalisz, Poland, and State University of Applied Sciences, Konin, Poland. His research interests include form-focused instruction, corrective feedback, learner autonomy, learning strategies, motivation, willingness to communicate, emotions in L2 learning and teaching, study abroad and pronunciation teaching.

New Directions in Computer Assisted Language Learning
Series Editors: Mark Peterson and Mariusz Kruk

Understanding Emotions in English Language Learning in Virtual Worlds
Mariusz Kruk and Mirosław Pawlak

Understanding Emotions in English Language Learning in Virtual Worlds

Mariusz Kruk and Mirosław Pawlak

LONDON AND NEW YORK

First published 2022
by Routledge
4 Park Square, Milton Park, Abingdon, Oxon OX14 4RN

and by Routledge
605 Third Avenue, New York, NY 10158

Routledge is an imprint of the Taylor & Francis Group, an informa business

© 2022 Mariusz Kruk, Mirosław Pawlak

The right of Mariusz Kruk and Mirosław Pawlak to be identified as authors of this work has been asserted in accordance with sections 77 and 78 of the Copyright, Designs and Patents Act 1988.

All rights reserved. No part of this book may be reprinted or reproduced or utilised in any form or by any electronic, mechanical, or other means, now known or hereafter invented, including photocopying and recording, or in any information storage or retrieval system, without permission in writing from the publishers.

Trademark notice: Product or corporate names may be trademarks or registered trademarks, and are used only for identification and explanation without intent to infringe.

British Library Cataloguing-in-Publication Data
A catalogue record for this book is available from the British Library

Library of Congress Cataloging-in-Publication Data
Names: Kruk, Mariusz, 1971- author. | Pawlak, Mirosław, author.
Title: Understanding emotions in English language learning in virtual worlds / Mariusz Kruk, Mirosław Pawlak.
Description: Abingdon, Oxon ; New York, NY : Routledge, 2022. |
Series: New directions in CALL | Includes bibliographical references and index.
Identifiers: LCCN 2021052973 (print) | LCCN 2021052974 (ebook) |
ISBN 9781032145945 (hardback) | ISBN 9781032145938 (paperback) |
ISBN 9781003240068 (ebook)
Subjects: LCSH: English language--Study and teaching--Computer-assisted instruction for foreign speakers. | English language--Study and teaching--Foreign speakers. | Second language acquisition--Psychological aspects. | Language and emotions.
Classification: LCC PE1128.3 K78 2022 (print) | LCC PE1128.3 (ebook) |
DDC 428.0078/5–dc23/eng/20211210
LC record available at https://lccn.loc.gov/2021052973
LC ebook record available at https://lccn.loc.gov/2021052974

ISBN: 978-1-032-14594-5 (hbk)
ISBN: 978-1-032-14593-8 (pbk)
ISBN: 978-1-003-24006-8 (ebk)

DOI: 10.4324/9781003240068

Typeset in Times New Roman
by Taylor & Francis Books

Contents

List of illustrations	vii

Introduction — 1

1 Positive and negative emotions: Overview of selected theoretical issues — 3

Introduction 3
The role of emotions in L2 teaching and learning in conventional settings and CALL 3
Positive emotions: curiosity and enjoyment 6
Negative emotions: boredom and anxiety 11
Conclusion 18

2 Research on positive and negative emotions in L2 learning and teaching in conventional settings and CALL — 19

Introduction 19
Research on positive and negative emotions in conventional settings 19
Research on positive and negative emotions in CALL settings 33
Conclusion 46

3 Methodology of the research project — 48

Introduction 48
Aims and research questions 49
Participants 49
Data collection instruments 53
Research procedures and activities in SL 56

vi *Contents*

Data analysis 57
Conclusion 59

4 Research findings   60

Introduction 60
Quantitative findings 60
Qualitative findings 75
Discussion 95
Limitations 104
Conclusion 105

Conclusion   106

Appendices   110

References   117
Index   130

Illustrations

Figures

3.1	Research procedures and activities in SL	56
4.1	Overall levels of self-reported language learning curiosity, enjoyment, boredom and anxiety for each group in SL	66
4.2	Overall self-reported levels of language learning curiosity, enjoyment, boredom and anxiety for individual learners in Group 1 in SL	68
4.3	Self-reported levels of language learning curiosity, enjoyment, boredom and anxiety in each session in SL: individual learners in Group 1	69
4.4	Overall self-reported levels of language learning curiosity, enjoyment, boredom and anxiety for individual learners in Group 2 in SL	71
4.5	Self-reported levels of language learning curiosity, enjoyment, boredom and anxiety in each session in SL: individual learners in Group 2	72
4.6	Overall self-reported levels of language learning curiosity, enjoyment, boredom and anxiety for individual learners in Group 3 in SL	74
4.7	Self-reported levels of language learning curiosity, enjoyment, boredom and anxiety in each session in SL: individual learners in Group 3	75

Tables

3.1	Participants of the study	51
3.2	The interpretation of mean scores for the levels of language learning curiosity, enjoyment, boredom and anxiety	57
3.3	Student narratives	58
4.1	The mean and standard deviation values for the positive and negative emotions for the entire group in traditional context	61

viii *List of illustrations*

4.2	The mean and standard deviation values for the positive and negative emotions in the case of individual students in traditional context	64
4.3	The mean and standard deviation values for the positive and negative emotions during the visits to SL	64
4.4	The mean and standard deviation values for self-reported positive and negative emotions in Group 1, Group 2 and Group 3 in SL	65
4.5	The mean and standard deviation values for self-reported levels of language learning curiosity, enjoyment, boredom and anxiety for individual learners in Group 1 in SL	67
4.6	The mean and standard deviation values for self-reported levels of language learning curiosity, enjoyment, boredom and anxiety for individual learners in Group 2 in SL	70
4.7	The mean and standard deviation values for self-reported levels of language learning curiosity, enjoyment, boredom and anxiety for individual learners in Group 3 in SL	73

Introduction

Emotions are part and parcel of people's lives. They accompany individuals every day in personal and professional issues, including the process of learning a foreign/second language (L2). One of the most investigated emotions in L2 research, both in traditional (e.g., L2 classrooms) and digital (e.g., virtual worlds) settings, is language anxiety (e.g., Arnold, 2007; Aydin, 2011; Dewaele et al., 2017; Horwitz et al., 1986; MacIntyre, 2017; MacIntyre & Gardner, 1989; Melchor-Couto, 2017). It should be noted, however, that with the advent of positive psychology, applied linguists have been encouraged to look beyond this negative emotion and explore a wide array of various feelings that people experience in the process of L2 learning (cf. Dewaele & Li, 2020). This has resulted in a significant growth in the number of emotion studies in the area of second language acquisition (SLA) over the past several years, with the effect that empirical investigations of this intriguing topic can be easily found in many SLA books and/or refereed journals.

It has to be noted, however, that despite the obvious interest in the role of emotions in overall literature devoted to L2 teaching and learning, the same trend can hardly be observed in the field of computer-assisted language learning (CALL). Although, as signaled above, language anxiety has been the favorite subject of empirical investigations by CALL researchers, only a handful of studies have been designed to investigate the negative emotion of boredom in the realm of CALL (e.g., Kruk, 2021a) and positive emotions such as enjoyment and curiosity have remained neglected to a large extent. This being the case, the overall purpose of this book is to take an important step towards filling this evident research gap concerning the emotional side of L2 learning in the domain of CALL. More specifically, the volume approaches the phenomena of positive (i.e., enjoyment and curiosity) and negative (i.e., boredom and language anxiety) emotions from interrelated theoretical, empirical and pedagogical perspectives in order to boost our understanding of these emotions and their role in the process of L2 teaching and learning in CALL environments, such as virtual worlds.

The book is composed of four chapters. Chapter 1 focuses on an overview of selected theoretical issues regarding positive and negative emotions, shedding light on the role of emotions in L2 teaching and learning in traditional

DOI: 10.4324/9781003240068-1

2 Introduction

settings and CALL. Moreover, definitions, types, dimensions and sources of the positive emotions of curiosity and enjoyment, as well as the negative emotions of boredom and anxiety, that is, the four emotions investigated in the study whose results are presented in Chapter 4, are discussed. Chapter 2 shifts the focus to an overview of state-of-the-art research relating to positive and negative emotions in L2 learning and teaching in traditional contexts and CALL, with particular emphasis on research projects concerning the four emotions that are the focus of the study reported in Chapter 4. The following two chapters, that is, Chapter 3 and Chapter 4, are concerned with the methodology, findings of the research project, and discussion of these findings, attempting to elucidate the dynamics of the experience of the four investigated emotions, their relationships, factors causing them, but also addressing a number of limitations of the conducted study. Finally, the conclusion to the volume concisely summarizes the main results of the study, offers a handful of pedagogical recommendations that could maximize and minimize the occurrence of positive and negative emotions, respectively, in digital contexts, and discusses the directions of future research regarding emotions in L2 learning and teaching in CALL settings, both with respect to their goals and methodology.

1 Positive and negative emotions
Overview of selected theoretical issues

Introduction

The main aim of this chapter is to provide a brief overview of the theoretical underpinnings of empirical investigations into emotions in the domain of second language (L2) learning. Section 1 begins with a general discussion of the role of emotions, both positive and negative, in teaching and learning an L2 in traditional and computer-assisted language learning (CALL) contexts. Section 2 is devoted to an overview of theoretical issues regarding the positive emotions of curiosity and enjoyment, which are the two positive emotions investigated in the study reported in Chapter 4. This section begins with the presentation of the definitions of the emotions in question, their types and/or dimensions as well as their sources. The third section is dedicated to the negative emotions of boredom and anxiety, that is, the main negative emotions under investigation in the research project whose findings are presented in Chapter 4. In this section, the concepts of boredom and language anxiety are discussed in light of theories expounding on their definitions, typologies and sources.

The role of emotions in L2 teaching and learning in conventional settings and CALL

According to Reeve (2005, p. 294), "emotions are short-lived, feeling-arousal purposive-expressive phenomena that help us adapt to the opportunities and challenges we face during important life events." Emotions can also be described as the desirable or undesirable domain non-specific, socially mediated reactions experienced in a positive (pleasant) and/or negative (unpleasant) way (Dewaele & Pavelescu, 2021; Feldman Barrett, 2017; MacIntyre & Gregersen, 2012). MacIntyre and Gregersen (2012, p. 193) argue that "positive emotion facilitates the building of resources because positive emotion tends to broaden a person's perspective, opening the individual to absorb the language … negative emotion produces the opposite tendency, a narrowing of focus and a restriction of the range of potential language input." Positive emotions carry a pleasant subjective feeling (e.g., joy and happiness) but negative emotions involve an unpleasant

DOI: 10.4324/9781003240068-2

4 *Positive and negative emotions*

subjective feeling (e.g., sadness and fear) (Fredrickson, 1998, 2001, 2003). Emotional reactions occur from an aroused state of an individual and generate physiological changes that are accompanied by certain feelings and memories that predispose individuals to act in certain ways (Goleman, 2001, 2006). While on the surface negative emotions may appear to be superfluous as they prevent individuals from acting productively and/or effectively, the matter is more complicated than it might seem at first glance. This is because "positive emotion has a different function from negative emotion; they are not opposite ends of the same spectrum" (MacIntyre & Gregersen, 2012, p. 193) and they constitute two qualitatively different aspects of experience (Plutchik, 1980). Another important consideration is that in specific situations negative emotions may lead to positive outcomes, while positive emotions may result in negative consequences. This might be visible, for example, in the case of anger, which in some circumstances might trigger improved performance on a competitive task (Tamir & Bigman, 2014). By contrast, happiness may sometimes generate loneliness or depression if it is sought too intensively (Gruber et al., 2011).

Emotions are part and parcel of what transpires in the classroom as they jointly shape the process of L2 learning and teaching. It is quite surprising, then, that for many decades second language acquisition (SLA) researchers focused almost entirely on the negative emotion of anxiety, especially since the publication of the Foreign Language Classroom Anxiety Scale developed by Horwitz and her colleagues (Horwitz et al., 1986). The affective role of anxiety was investigated in connection with willingness to communicate, followed by research studies that brought other emotions into the picture, including enjoyment, frustration or hope (Imai, 2010). Other studies related to emotions in language learning were conducted as well, such as those carried out by Schumann (1997), who utilized neurological and psychological exposure to stimulus material in order to shed new light on the role of affect; Arnold (1999), who studied emotion (or affect) in relation to self-esteem, reflective learning, anxiety and autonomy; or Norton (2000), who considered the role of identity. As argued by Noels, Pon and Clément (1996), emotions play a substantial role in researching language learner identity, since learning an additional language can be an intense emotional experience as it inevitably takes place at the intersection of language, culture and identity. Of importance are also the psychological dimensions of L2 learning with respect to multilingualism and the divergent ways in which emotions are exhibited by multilinguals (Dewaele, 2005, 2011), as well as Bown and White's (2010) social cognitive model of emotion in L2 learning, which helps to understand the role of emotions in this endeavor, highlighting the social antecedents of emotions, the significance of cognitive appraisals of situations, as well as the regulation of emotion.

The positive psychology movement has also had an important role to play in emotion research in the field of SLA (Wang et al., 2021). Positive psychology, defined by Fredrickson (2001, p. 218) as development of the ability to "understand and foster the factors that allow individuals, communities, and societies to flourish," inspired research into positive emotions (MacIntyre & Mercer, 2014). The role of enjoyment in learning an L2 was confirmed in the study carried out by Dewaele and MacIntyre (2014), who investigated this positive emotion together with foreign language anxiety. They found that language learners experienced less anxiety than enjoyment, and that the latter played a more important role as it appeared to be more meaningful to the participants. Ross and Stracke (2016) explored the emotion of pride among tertiary language learners in Australian universities with regard to the situated learning environment of the language classroom and authentic out-of-class social interaction. The results showed a considerable role of pride in the language classroom context, primarily as a consequence of good grades or praise from peers, although the students did not feel pride in reaction to successful task performance when no rewards were offered. Pride also played an important part in communicative settings outside the classroom, where the participants experienced this positive emotion more frequently and did not expect rewards. The positive emotion of hope was investigated by Ross and Rivers (2018) among university-level Australian learners in their English-speaking out-of-class context. The researchers showed that hope was not at all linked to the students' formal learning environment, but was related to their future ability and willingness to confidently and effortlessly use a language in naturalistic settings for communicative purposes. Yet another positive emotion, love, was examined in the studies conducted by Pavelescu and Petrić (2018), and Barcelos (2021). In the former, love turned out to be the driving force of L2 learning and by itself motivated the participants to look for ways of overcoming the difficulties they faced and to put more effort into their learning. In the latter study, love constituted an important element of the participant's identity as a prospective teacher of English as a foreign language (EFL), nurturing her inner and interpersonal peace needed for both herself and her future students.

As mentioned above, negative emotions constitute an integral part of learning an L2. Although SLA research has been preoccupied with the negative emotion of anxiety for many decades, resulting in the fact that other negative emotions experienced by language learners have largely been overlooked in the SLA literature, recent studies, albeit still few in number, have also focused on such negative emotions as shame, guilt, anger and boredom. To begin with, the negative role of shame was investigated by Galmiche (2017), who found that it was the most commonly reported negative emotion when compared to anxiety and frustration. The feeling of shame reduced the learners' linguistic confidence, their perception of identity, and self-esteem. As for guilt, this negative emotion (along with shame) was the focus of the study carried out by Teimouri (2018) among EFL learners. The results showed that guilt was found to positively correlate with the students' motivation and their language achievement, while shame was strongly and negatively linked to these two variables. Cook's (2006) mixed-methods study explored the effect of shame and anxiety in learning the

6 *Positive and negative emotions*

English language. The researcher reported that multiple shame episodes were primarily sparked by the students' sensed deficiency in their target language (TL) ability. The observed shame-anger sequence revealed that the shame the learners felt culminated in reliance on anger as a strategy of defence. Finally, Kruk and Zawodniak (2018) showed that feelings of boredom were triggered by teacher-imposed topics, an unchallenging, repetitive nature of the tasks performed, teacher personality and the discrepancy between language activities used and the students' level of English proficiency.

As can be seen, the role of emotions in conventional settings has changed due to the introduction of positive psychology into SLA research, which resulted in a shift from "the exclusive preoccupation with learners' anxiety to the inclusion of both positive and negative classroom emotions" (Dewaele & Li, 2020, p. 37). It should be noted, however, that the same trend has hardly been mirrored in the realm of computer-assisted language learning (CALL). This is because, for many decades, primary importance in this setting has been attached to the negative emotion of language anxiety. In fact, only recently have the aversive emotion of boredom and other emotions (e.g., enjoyment) and their roles in teaching and learning an L2 in digital settings been brought to the fore. With respect to anxiety, CALL researchers, for example, uncovered a decrease in the effect of this negative emotion in a stress-free learning environment generated by means of CALL technologies (e.g., Ataiefar & Sadighi, 2017; Bashori et al., 2020; Freiermuth & Jarrell, 2006; Kartal & Balçikanlı, 2018; Kissau et al., 2010; Roed, 2003; Satar & Özdener, 2008). As regards boredom, the role of this negative emotion (also in conjunction with language anxiety) has mainly been explored in the field of the virtual world of Second Life (SL; e.g., Kruk, 2019, 2021a, 2021b), and also in studies carried out by Li and Dewaele (2020) as well as Derakhshan and colleagues (Derakhshan et al., 2021), who explored the role boredom played in connection with the use of online learning platforms. These studies showed that the experience of boredom (as well as language anxiety) was generated by a host of factors that prevented the participants from taking full advantage of these digital platforms. When it comes to research that involved positive emotions, Yoshida (2020a) found that enjoyment was the most often occurring positive emotion during online text chats in Japanese with Japanese native speakers, while a feeling of difficulty was the most frequent negative emotion. While the chat process and issues with the Japanese language played a role in generating negative emotions, the chat partners, conversations about hobbies, shared interests, and culture played a part in evoking positive emotions (for a thorough overview of studies on positive and negative emotions in L2 learning in CALL, see Chapter 2).

Positive emotions: curiosity and enjoyment

The present section is dedicated to the positive emotions of curiosity and enjoyment, that is, the two positive emotions that are the focus of the study whose results are offered in Chapter 4. This section commences with a

Positive and negative emotions 7

presentation of the relevant definitions of curiosity, including language learning curiosity, its types and sources. This is followed by a discussion of pertinent definitions of enjoyment, different dimensions and sources of this positive emotion.

Curiosity

In view of the fact that curiosity is one of the least frequently examined positive emotion in L2 contexts (Mahmoodzadeh & Khajavy, 2019), the construct needs to be approached from a more psychological perspective and elucidated on the basis of different theories and models such as *optimal arousal* (Spielberger & Starr, 1994), *dynamic subsystem regulation* (Iran-Nejad & Cecil, 1992) or *information-gap* (Loewenstein, 1994). For example, in optimal arousal theories, curiosity is viewed as a pleasant experience in which individuals pursue an appropriate degree of novelty (i.e., the level should not be too high/low so as not to trigger anxiety or boredom) (Spielberger & Starr, 1994). In the knowledge-gap model, curiosity results from the recognition of unknown chunks of information, which makes an individual experience a strong yearning for closure, giving rise to information search (Loewenstein, 1994). Broadly speaking, curiosity is the longing for new information, knowledge and experiences as well as an incentive to resolve gaps and/or experience the unknown (Arnone & Grabowsky, 1992; Grossnickle, 2016; Litman, 2005). Curiosity has a considerable influence on thoughts, feelings and behavior (Spielberger & Reheiser, 2009), which manifests itself as "a desire for new information aroused by novel, complex, or ambiguous stimuli" (Litman & Jimerson 2004, p. 147). Curiosity can also be described dynamically, as an attribute which, depending on context, can rise or fall, and thus be similar to physical hunger (Lau et al., 2018) or it can be perceived as a psychological variable, a dynamic trait-like one, which, depending on a situation, differs among individuals (Arnone et al., 1994). Of particular interest to the present book is the understanding of the construct of curiosity in the field of SLA. According to Mahmoodzadeh and Khajavy (2019, p. 336), curiosity can be characterized as "a possible drive generating and maintaining the willingness to learn and use a foreign language … an affective-cognitive variable specific to language learning which reflects an inquiry-driven interest and desire to learn and use a foreign language."

The literature distinguishes various types of curiosity, of which the most relevant are the crucial distinctions between *state* and *trait* curiosity, *perceptual* and *epistemic* curiosity, *interest-type* (I-type) curiosity and *deprivation-type* (D-type) curiosity, as well as *specific/diversive* curiosity and *breadth/depth* curiosity. As for the first distinction, state curiosity is regarded as a transient condition, a momentary experience occurring in specific situations arising in an individual's environment (i.e., curiosity is stimulated by different variables such as novelty or complexity). In contrast, trait curiosity is a general propensity, or, in other words, it is a relatively enduring

8 *Positive and negative emotions*

personality trait (i.e., it persists across a number of situations). It should be noted, however, that the two types of curiosity are found to be closely related, indicating that individuals can now and then experience certain situations that prompt a state of curiosity, irrespective of the level of their trait curiosity (Grossnickle, 2016). Moving on to the distinction between perceptual and epistemic curiosity (Loewenstein, 1994), the former relates to a sensory experience triggered by visual, auditory or tactile stimuli (Litman, 2005; Litman & Spielberger, 2003), whereas the latter is specifically germane to education (Loewenstein, 1994) since it constitutes "a desire for knowledge that motivates individuals to learn new ideas, eliminate information gaps, and solve intellectual problems" (Litman, 2008, p. 1586). It should also be noted that epistemic curiosity is further categorized into *interpersonal* and *intrapersonal*, with the former being motivated by a desire to gain new information about other persons' feelings and/or experiences (Litman & Pezzo, 2007), and the latter involving inquisitive introspection in order to obtain a deeper insight into one's inner self (Litman et al., 2017). Litman and colleagues (Litman, 2010; Litman et al., 2010; Litman & Jimerson, 2004) further distinguish interest-type (I-type) curiosity and deprivation-type (D-type) curiosity. I-type curiosity is linked to positive affective responses related to information seeking that is enjoyable to an individual and may stimulate interest. For I-type curiosity, gaps in knowledge act as positive incentives to be pursued and subsequently filled in some way as a result of the satisfaction from learning something new (Grossnickle, 2016). In contrast, D-type curiosity involves "a motive to reduce unpleasant experiences of feeling deprived of new knowledge" (Lauriola et al., 2015, p. 202). Importantly, both I-type curiosity and D-type curiosity are positively related to acquisition of knowledge (Rotgans & Schmidt, 2014), performance in schools (Eren & Coskun, 2016) or self-regulation (Lauriola et al., 2015). As regards specific and diversive types of curiosity, they relate to whether the purpose of curiosity is to lessen uncertainty or to intensify arousal by pursuing uncertainty, respectively (Spielberger & Starr, 1994). Finally, breadth and depth concentrate on whether the object of curiosity is a choice of topics that is broad or narrow (Grossnickle, 2016).

Of paramount importance to the present book is the conceptualization of language learning curiosity (LLC), proposed by Mahmoodzadeh and Khajavy (2019). It is based on Litman and Jimerson's (2004) *interest-deprivation (I/D) theory of curiosity*, which posits that inquisitive thinking and exploratory behavior can be influenced by stimulation and diminution of curiosity. Since, according to Mahmoodzadeh and Khajavy (2019, p. 336), "language learners show a distinct kind of curiosity that generates and maintains interest, enjoyment, and willingness to learn in language learning contexts because they are already familiar with at least one native language system in its entirety," the researchers utilized the aforementioned framework of the I/D model of curiosity and theorized two orientations of LLC: (1) *language curiosity as a feeling-of-interest* (LCFI) and (2) *language curiosity as a feeling-of-deprivation* (LCFD). In view of the fact that LCFI is linked to the positive feelings of interest and enjoyment induced in L2 learners who curiously look for opportunities to use a language for the purpose of communication, Mahmoodzadeh and Khajavy categorized it as *L2 communicative curiosity*. As for LCFD, this orientation is viewed as "a strong curiosity-driven desire for a feeling-of-knowing that motivates the information-seeking behavior and the eagerness to fulfilling the gap knowledge in a new L2 system" (Mahmoodzadeh & Khajavy, 2019, p. 336) and as such it was classified as *linguistic curiosity*. Importantly, the researchers posit that these two orientations are not mutually exclusive but, rather, are complementary in the process of learning an L2.

As can be seen from the foregoing discussion, curiosity, in general, can be triggered by a number of factors. Among other things, they include craving knowledge, new information (Kang et al., 2009; Litman, 2010); searching for variation (Loewenstein, 1994); features of the environment (Loewenstein, 1994); searching for opportunities to be curious (Kashdan et al., 2004; Litman & Silvia, 2006); new experiences and uncertainty seeking (Arnone & Grabowsky, 1992; Kashdan et al., 2009); and the need to obtain new information with the aim of enjoyment and/or interest or the desire to reduce the unknown or the feeling of ignorance (Litman, 2005). In addition, research shows that curiosity may be invoked by incomplete information replete with information gaps (Shin & Kim, 2019), teacher support and peer influence (Zhao et al., 2011), personal interest in the subject and interesting elements of lessons (Palmer, 2018), and classroom activities, peers, cognitive puzzles and the communicative environment of the L2 classroom (Nakamura et al., 2020).

Enjoyment

When it comes to enjoyment, in stark contrast to curiosity, it is a frequently investigated positive emotion in the context of language learning. The concept of Foreign Language Enjoyment (FLE) was introduced into the field of SLA by Dewaele and MacIntyre (2014). Enjoyment is defined as "a positive affective state that combines challenge, happiness, interest, fun, sense of pride, and sense of meaning" (Dewaele & Li, 2021) and is viewed as "a complex and relatively stable emotion" (Dewaele & Li, 2020). This positive emotion is, however, different from pleasure (Csikszentmihalyi, 2004). This is because FLE is

> a complex emotion, capturing interacting dimensions of challenge and perceived ability that reflect the human drive for success in the face of difficult tasks ... On the one hand, enjoyments occur when people not only meet their needs, but exceed them to accomplish something new or even unexpected; on the other hand, pleasure is a simpler feeling that something likable is happening.
>
> (Dewaele & MacIntyre, 2016, pp. 216–217)

10 *Positive and negative emotions*

The distinction between the two concepts is further explained by Boudreau, MacIntyre and Dewaele (2018), who comment: "If pleasure can occur simply by performing an activity or completing an action, enjoyment takes on additional dimensions such as an intellectual focus, heightened attention, and optimal challenge" (p. 153).

Research has uncovered a variety of dimensions of FLE. The study conducted by Dewaele and MacIntyre (2016) revealed two dimensions of this construct: (1) a social dimension and (2) a private dimension. The social dimension was linked with nice and encouraging teachers and peers as well as a positive classroom environment, as indicated by the quantitative analysis of the data loading on the identified factor (i.e., the FLE-Social), which included words and/or phrases such as "laugh," "tight group," "nice," "encouraging," "supporting," "a good atmosphere" and "a positive environment" (Dewaele & MacIntyre, 2016, p. 231). This social dimension of FLE was also identified in the qualitative analysis of the data when participants pointed to such issues as positive events in the classroom, respect for the needs and weaknesses of learners shown by their teachers, teachers' thoughtful praise, as well as the teachers' mood and their ability to understand the emotional classroom atmosphere. As for the private dimension, it concerned the cognition that accompanies FLE and a feeling of achievement. The dimension in question was identified in the quantitative analysis as the FLE-Private factor and was characterized by such words/phrases as "feel proud," "enjoy it" or "it's fun" (Dewaele & MacIntyre, 2016, p. 231). In addition, qualitative analysis showed the relevance of personal success (despite obstacles) and teaching techniques (however risky they could be). In another study by Li et al. (2018), quantitative analysis allowed identification of three dimensions of FLE: (1) FLE-Private, (2) FLE-Teacher and (3) FLE-Atmosphere. The first dimension highlighted personal progress, excellent language performance and pride derived from it, interest, novelty, positive changes, the use of the target language in interactions with peers, the experience of flow, and understanding of the language produced by both teachers and other students. The second dimension, that is, FLE-Teacher, was connected with pedagogical practices and the enjoyable experiences concerning supportive and encouraging attitudes towards students manifested by teachers, teachers' praise and their personal attention, their involvement in learners' concerns, as well as the utilization of non-traditional instructional techniques or strategies. As far as the third dimension (i.e., FLE-Atmosphere) is concerned, it emphasized teacher-controlled group activities that triggered learners' positive engagement. Similar dimensions of FLE were reported by Botes et al. (2020a), who emphasized the role of the teacher in establishing a positive foreign language classroom environment, as well as personal and social enjoyment of learning a foreign language, with the latter being explicitly related to the social cohesion and solidarity with classmates. Finally, worth mentioning also are the three dimensions of FLE identified by Jin and Zhang (2021). They included: (1) enjoyment of teacher support, (2) enjoyment of English learning and (3) enjoyment of student support.

Besides the above-discussed dimensions of FLE, which, on the one hand, reveal the multidimensionality of the construct, and, on the other hand, indicate sources of FLE, it is possible to enumerate a number of additional triggers of enjoyment in the language classroom. These include, among others, attitudes towards the target language and the target language culture (e.g., De Smet et al., 2018; Dewaele & Dewaele, 2017; Dewaele et al., 2019; Dewaele & Proietti Ergün, 2020), the role of the teacher (i.e., frequency of use of the target language, teacher unpredictability, his or her friendliness, teacher perception) (e.g., Dewaele et al., 2018; Jiang & Dewaele, 2019; Dewaele et al., 2019; Dewaele & MacIntyre, 2019; Teimouri et al., 2020), school context (i.e., status of the target language) (De Smet et al., 2018), societal context (De Smet et al., 2018), self-factors (i.e., age, sex) (e.g., Dewaele et al., 2018; Dewaele et al, 2019; Dewaele & MacIntyre, 2014), multilingualism (Botes et al., 2020b; Dewaele & MacIntyre, 2014; Dewaele et al., 2019), cultural empathy (Dewaele & MacIntyre, 2019), and target language proficiency (e.g., Botes et al., 2020a; Dewaele & Alfawazan, 2018; Dewaele et al., 2018; Dewaele & MacIntyre, 2014; Mierzwa, 2018). Last but not least, the occurrence of enjoyment in the process of L2 learning is influenced by the degree of students' autonomy as well as by whether they are given opportunities to seek novelty and pursue challenging goals (Dewaele & MacIntyre, 2014).

Negative emotions: boredom and anxiety

The focus of the present section is on the negative emotions of boredom and anxiety, that is, the two aversive emotions that, along with the positive emotions of curiosity and enjoyment, are the subject of investigation of the research project, the outcomes of which are reported in Chapter 4. This section begins with a discussion of the pertinent definitions of boredom, including the ones related to teaching and learning an L2, the presentation of different types of this negative emotion, and an overview of existing theories and models of boredom along with its sources. Subsequently the discussion will be shifted to the outline of germane definitions of language anxiety, the investigation of major approaches to the phenomenon in question, its types and sources.

Boredom

Boredom is a complex, multifaceted and multidimensional construct including various elements and resulting from numerous causes (cf. Ally, 2008; Caldwell et al., 1999; Pawlak et al., 2020c) and thus difficult to define. In light of the equivocal and complex nature of boredom, it can be considered from psychological and social/sociological perspectives (Weinerman & Kenner, 2016). When looking at boredom through a psychological lens, the construct is understood as an affective phenomenon, trait- (enduring) or state-like (transitory) in nature, which may hinder the process of learning in a serious way (Acee et al., 2010; Daniels et al., 2015; Goetz et al., 2010; Nett et al.,

12 *Positive and negative emotions*

2010). In the field of sociology, boredom is viewed as a crucial component of personality embraced for the purpose of defying the rules and restrictions established and imposed by the educational system (Brumhead et al., 1990; Larson & Richards, 1991). To put it simply, the mechanism of boredom is activated when young people find it hard to acknowledge the system of values in the adult world, to which they react with diverse manifestations of this aversive emotion.

The multifarious qualities of boredom are best reflected in the definition provided by Fahlman (2009), who described it as an emotion, a feeling, an affect, a drive, attention deficit, altered time perception, diminished vitality, a phenomenon that "can be experienced across varying durations of time" (Fahlman, 2009, p. 54). She refers to it as the pivotal issue of an individual's desire for engagement in activity of appropriate quantity and quality, and the dissatisfaction that this engagement is not happening. It is worth noting, then, that disengagement, which results in lower performance and obstructs the learning process, is one of the components of boredom (Fahlman, 2009; Pekrun et al., 2010). As far as the field of SLA is concerned, boredom can be defined as a subjective state of not being engaged in language tasks given by language teachers that may be experienced with changing levels of intensity, contingent on learners' predispositions and preferences as well as diverse situational factors (Zawodniak & Kruk, 2018a). It can also be described in this context as "a state of disengagement caused by lack of interest and involvement" (Kruk et al., 2021, p. 21). Worth mentioning also is the definition of boredom in the context of learning an L2 provided by Li, Dewaele and Hu (2021), who understand the construct as "a negative emotion with an extremely low degree of activation/arousal that arises from ongoing activities [which are] typically over-challenging or under-challenging and/or of little significance, relevance, or meaning to the learners" (p. 12). Although it is a challenge to define boredom and tease it apart from similar constructs, like demotivation and disengagement (Mercer & Dörnyei, 2020), the diverse nature of this aversive emotion, shown in the definitions provided above, contributes to its distinctiveness (Daniels et al., 2015).

In view of the fact that boredom is the most intense and the most frequently experienced academic emotion that students experience in a variety of subjects, including foreign language learning, it is warranted to take a look at various types of the construct in question that have been proposed by different authors, mainly those from outside the field of SLA. Neu (1998) distinguishes between *endogenous* boredom and *reactive* boredom, with the former being derived from the inside of an individual and the latter being caused by what is happening in his or her environment. Acee et al. (2010) divide boredom into *task-focused* (i.e., boredom that is associated with situations where students are requested to perform tasks they consider meaningless) and *self-focused* (i.e., boredom that refers to frustration-stimulating learning situations). Boredom can also be considered as *state* boredom (i.e., it is referred to as a situation-specific experience) and *trait* boredom (i.e., it is viewed as a more general disposition attributed to

Positive and negative emotions 13

individuals). More specifically, state boredom can be portrayed as a momentary, context-dependent, ephemeral condition derived from an individual's observation that his or her learning milieu is not interesting and not sufficiently arousing (Bench & Lench, 2013; Fahlman, 2009). As a result, individuals can experience this type of boredom, when, for instance, teachers do not select topics and/or activities adjusted to learners' expectations, abilities and proficiency levels. In addition, state boredom is the consequence of low arousal that is generated by lack of interest, lack of satisfaction, or frustration. It can also fluctuate across time and create problems in focusing on tasks to be performed. It is worth noting, however, that, as indicated by some specialists (e.g., Vogel-Walcutt et al., 2012), state boredom results not only from reduced energy but also from increased, situation-specific stimulation. While this type of boredom is an undesirable psychological condition, it can be averted and turned into a stimulating experience of looking for different objectives and efficient ways of confronting such unwanted situations (Sharp et al., 2017; Vogel-Walcutt et al., 2012). As far as trait boredom is concerned, it is an integral component of personality, characteristic of individuals who tend to display a greater disposition to succumb to this negative emotion, which leads to perpetual disinterest and disengagement. Trait boredom can further be subdivided into *external* (i.e., an inclination to perceive the immediate environment as unengaging, which results in seeking novelty and thrill) and *internal* (i.e., an incapacity to find and do interesting things) boredom proneness (Macklem, 2015). Students who are more prone to experience boredom exhibit a general inclination to manifest negative emotions, which, among other things, cause a diminution in motivation, self-regulating learning, willingness to speak, activation of cognitive resources and achievement (Götz et al., 2006). Trait boredom is also believed to cause student stress, understood as a state of mental strain that emerges from different adverse and/or perplexing situations (Berryhill et al., 2009).

Another set of boredom types pertains to the intensity of this negative emotion, as proposed by Goetz et al. (2014). This typology portrays the emotion in question as multiple boredoms, which encompass *indifferent* boredom, *calibrating* boredom, *searching* boredom, *reactant* boredom and *apathetic* boredom. Each type is discussed from the perspective of different levels of (un)pleasantness of this emotion. As for indifferent boredom, it is described as a pleasant state of calmness and withdrawal. It is most commonly experienced by students in their free time. This emotion is exhibited through an impartial attitude to the surroundings, slightly positive valence and low levels of arousal. Calibrating boredom is a moderately unpleasant state of scattered thoughts. This state makes students unable and unwilling to focus on a given task. Although they do not like such a disposition and want to change it, they do not know how to attain this objective. As regards searching boredom, it is experienced in an unpleasant way by restless but creative individuals. They are displeased with the situation they are in and want to change it by looking for occasions for doing something different. Reactant boredom is a severely unpleasant and aversive emotion

14 *Positive and negative emotions*

characteristic of individuals who urgently seek ways to avoid it, which generates anger and aggressive behaviors. This gives rise to deflecting blame for being bored onto various external factors (e.g., teachers, topics, learning materials). Finally, apathetic boredom is the most severe subtype of boredom in which this feeling becomes so intense that students become numb and display indifference to the situation they have found themselves in. Expanding on the subtypes of boredom just discussed, Van Tilburg and Igou (2011) suggested that searching boredom (unlike the other four subtypes of boredom, which alienate students from their passions, interests and desires) may function as a motivating trigger and offer students an opportunity to seek new challenges and recognize their goals.

The "complex and obscure" nature of boredom (Zawodniak et al., 2021, p. 2) can be elucidated by models and theories of the construct that also highlight some of its sources. The *under-stimulation model* (Larson & Richards, 1991) asserts that boredom is induced by the lack of new stimuli that could make individuals pursue new goals and explore the environment that surrounds them. According to the model, if learners are directly instructed what to do and, instead of problem-solving activities, they are expected to rely on rote learning, it is likely that they will disengage and consequently boredom will ensue. In the *forced-effort model* (Hill & Perkins, 1985; Pekrun et al., 2010), making learners invest mental energy in undertaking monotonous, repetitive and unchallenging activities is seen as the main source generating boredom. This usually occurs when teachers explicitly oversee all students' behavior, leaving them limited or no room for autonomy. Conversely, the *dimensional model* (Pekrun et al., 2010), besides considering the deactivating quality of boredom, also concentrates on the bright side of the emotion in question, that is, its activating potential. For example, when a student has felt boredom for a long time, his or her activity levels may show a growing tendency in reaction to efforts to maintain attention. In such circumstances, boredom can be viewed as a springboard for action to be taken and as a way to channel mental energy to more satisfying tasks in order to alleviate the situation. In fact, it could be argued that in this sense boredom can be considered as serving a motivating function (Tulis & Fulmer, 2013). Worth mentioning is also Pekrun's (1992) *cognitive-motivational model of emotion effects*, which asserts that the impact of academic emotions on individuals' achievement is caused by cognitive and motivational mechanisms. Here, negative academic emotions, including boredom, emasculate motivation and force students to fall back on inefficient cognitive strategies (e.g., rote learning). As far as the *attentional theory of boredom proneness* (Eastwood et al., 2007; Fisherl, 1993; Harris, 2000; LePera, 2011) is concerned, lack of concentration or failure to remain focused on uninteresting, unengaging learning activities is the central cause of boredom. In other words, if a particular task fails to meet learners' interests or expectations, they will need to generate self-sustained attention. Such a state of affairs will give them the impression that time is lengthened, resulting in the increased experience of boredom. According to the *control-value theory of achievement emotions* (Pekrun, 2006; Pekrun et al., 2010; Tulis & Fulmer, 2013),

Positive and negative emotions   15

sources of boredom are seen in learners who are not able to control a given task or find value in it. According to this theory, if learners' perception of a task is of low or no value, and if they feel compelled to complete it irrespective of whether they like it or not, then the most likely effect will be the emergence of unpleasant emotions, such as boredom, together with its avoidance behaviors, passivity and reduction of cognitive focus. In another theory, that is, the *emotion theory* (Eastwood et al., 2007), a student's alexithymic failure to recognize, access, comprehend and communicate his or her own feelings is seen as a crucial antecedent of boredom. Such emotional illiteracy is characteristic of externally oriented individuals. It makes the learning process an arduous and unsatisfactory experience filled with setbacks in identifying one's problems and solutions. In yet another theory, that is, the *menton theory of engagement and boredom* (Davies & Fortney, 2012), cognitive processing required for performance of a task necessitates the utilization of mentons (i.e., mental energy units). According to this theory, both an individual's deficit or surplus of mentons may generate the feeling of boredom. In other words, an individual can experience boredom as a consequence of being exposed to over- and/or under-challenging tasks. In this case, boredom may play a positive role in motivating him or her to search for new stimuli and productively use the excess mentons. Finally, boredom can also be considered in terms of *component theories of emotional experiences* (Kleinginna & Kleinginna, 1981; Scherer, 2000). Within this conceptualization, boredom is a type of emotion comprising five components: affective (undesired feelings), cognitive (attention deficit), expressive (getting restless), motivational (retreating from continuing a task) and physiological (insufficient levels of arousal).

As can be seen from the above overview of different models and theories of boredom, this negative emotion may be caused by such factors as the absence of new stimuli, the focus on uninteresting and unengaging tasks, the inability to recognize and communicate one's own feelings, or being over- and/or under-challenged. In addition, the literature shows that feelings of boredom may be triggered by unclear or ill-defined objectives that can pose a daunting challenge to attain, as well as a variety of institutional constrictions that may hamper the learning process and render it uninvolving (Vogel-Walcutt et al., 2012; Weinerman & Kenner, 2016). Other contributors to boredom may include uninteresting and overly easy tasks, which can diminish student involvement and compel bored individuals to behave as evaders, escaping participation in unchallenging tasks and doing something else (Daniels et al., 2015; Nett et al., 2010). Feelings of boredom may also be influenced by, surprisingly, attractive and well-designed tasks, when, for example, learners might not be permitted to select topics (Patall, 2013). Finally, boredom may also arise from a lack of activity that could give students pleasure and enjoyment and, hence, they perceive the learning milieu as meaningless (Eastwood et al., 2012). Although limited to a handful of studies related to the experience of boredom in the context of CALL, or more specifically, the virtual world of Second Life, relevant literature shows that the feelings of boredom may emerge from

16   *Positive and negative emotions*

uninteresting conversations, unwillingness to interact with interlocutors, comprehension problems, monotony, meeting boring, rude or aggressive users, as well as the scarcity of conversation topics (Kruk, 2016a, 2019, 2021a, 2021b).

Anxiety

Learning an L2 is a highly complex process that inevitably entails a range of different affective states or emotions. One of them is anxiety, which in a wider sense, can be understood as "the subjective feeling of tension, apprehension, nervousness, and worry associated with an arousal of the autonomic nervous system" (Spielberger, 1983, p. 15). In the field of SLA, this negative emotion is defined as "a distinct complex of self-perceptions, beliefs, feelings, and behaviors related to classroom language learning arising from the uniqueness of the language learning process" (Horwitz et al., 1986, p. 128). This distinctiveness stems from the fact that L2 learners are expected to use a language that they still have to master, and the language they produce is continually evaluated by the teacher, that is, the most proficient speaker in the classroom, but also, possibly other students. In such circumstances, they constantly feel tension, uncertainty and frustration (Horwitz et al., 1986; Piechurska-Kuciel, 2011a). In addition, this negative emotion is accompanied by a variety of psycho-physiological symptoms that may include tension, tremor, perspiration, elevated pulse, forgetfulness or avoidance behaviors (Horwitz et al., 1986). Of particular importance to the study reported later in the present book is the recent definition of the phenomenon offered by MacIntyre (2017). He describes anxiety as

> an emotion that fluctuates over time and that might be examined on a timescale of seconds and minutes, as in the rising and falling of anxiety during communication, or a timescale of days, as in fluctuations during a week of classes, or a timescale of months/years, as in the trajectory of anxiety across the years of a language programme.
>
> (MacIntyre, 2017, pp. 22–23)

The general conceptualization of anxiety differentiates between *state* anxiety and *trait* anxiety. While the former type functions on a temporary basis as it concerns a particular situation and point in time, the latter is an attribute of a person's character or his or her propensity to feel anxious (Ellis, 2008; MacIntyre, 1995, 2017; Woodrow, 2006). In addition, in the field of SLA a type of *situation-specific* anxiety can be distinguished that highlights the complex character of this negative emotion (MacIntyre & Gardner, 1991). Anxiety of this type is linked with assessing certain events as anxiety-inducing, for example, when a language learner feels perplexed answering his or her teacher's question and expects the embarrassment occurring yet again (MacIntyre, 2017). Anxiety is also further divided into *facilitating* and *debilitating* (Alpert & Haber, 1960; Ellis, 2008; Scovel, 1978). While the former motivates an individual to increase his or her efforts to perform better during a new task, the latter forces a student to abandon an activity in order to avoid anticipated failure (Scovel, 1991). As far as the internal structure of foreign language anxiety is concerned, it comprises three subcomponents: (1) communication apprehension, (2) test anxiety and (3) fear of negative evaluation (Horwitz et al., 1986). Of paramount importance to the L2 classroom is the first of them, that is, communication apprehension, as it involves the actual use of the target language (TL). This is because language learners commonly experience speaking difficulties arising from the fact that they have limited control over communicative situations and acute awareness that they are subjected to evaluation. Communication apprehension further involves oral communication anxiety (i.e., related to speaking in pairs or groups), "stage fright" (i.e., concerning speaking in public) and receiver anxiety (i.e., regarding facing problems with comprehending a spoken message) (Horwitz et al., 1986).

There are three major approaches to investigating foreign language anxiety, as identified by MacIntyre (2017): (1) *confounded*, (2) *specialized* and (3) *dynamic*. As regards the first one, it refers to studies that elicit anxiety-related notions that originate from a broad range of sources without giving particular attention to the occurrence of anxiety in the L2 classroom. Within the confounded approach, researchers primarily depend on psychological measures of anxiety. When it comes to the specialized approach, it focuses on situation-specific anxiety, its pertinent definitions and notions, as well as anxiety-based studies. In this approach foreign language anxiety was conceptualized and a number of anxiety measures were developed. They include, for example, the French Classroom Anxiety and French Use Anxiety (Gardner, 1985), the Foreign Language Classroom Anxiety Scale (FLCAS; Horwitz et al., 1986), as well as scales concerning language anxiety at the input, processing and output stages created by MacIntyre and Gardner (1994). The approach in question concerns studies dedicated to uncovering relationships between anxiety and a host of learner variables such as perceived competence (e.g., MacIntyre et al., 1997), willingness to communicate (MacIntyre et al., 1997) or learner personality (e.g., Dewaele, 2002). The third approach, the dynamic one, relates to studies that set out to examine this negative emotion "in connection with a complex web of language experiences" (MacIntyre, 2017, p. 11) that dynamically interact with a number of individual difference (ID) factors. They include, for example, enjoyment, willingness to communicate, motivation and boredom (e.g., Boudreau et al., 2018; Gregersen et al., 2014; Kruk, 2019).

Language anxiety may be sparked by a host of sources. The most comprehensive list of such triggers, presented by Young (1991), includes (1) personal and interpersonal anxieties, (2) learner beliefs about L2 learning, (3) teacher beliefs about L2 teaching, (4) teacher-learner interactions, (5) classroom procedures and (6) L2 testing. The first source is influenced by low self-esteem, competitiveness or communication apprehension. It can also be impacted by social anxiety and anxiety specific to learning additional languages. The second source concerns learners' attention given to specific elements of

18 *Positive and negative emotions*

language learning (e.g., vocabulary, pronunciation, trips to countries where the target language is spoken) and to the belief that some individuals are more capable of learning an L2 than others. The third source pertains to such issues as the apparent responsibility for correcting all errors made by language learners, the lack of ability to control students when they work in pairs or groups, and the act of being the controller. As for the fourth source, it can be epitomized by language learners' uncertainty and apprehension related to the way in which their errors can be perceived by their teachers and peers. The fifth source of anxiety predominantly involves situations when students use the TL in front of their classmates or when they are called on to speak by the teacher. Finally, the sixth source concerns different test formats that may generate various levels of anxiety. When it comes to the CALL context, language anxiety may be triggered by different types of language activities, or more precisely, the focus on correctness and precision (Coryell & Clark, 2009), interaction with unfamiliar users, insufficient L2 competence, comprehension problems, the fear of making mistakes, or negative past experiences (e.g., Kruk, 2021b; 2021c).

Due to a variety of sources of language anxiety, the experience of this negative emotion in the L2 classroom may exert a negative impact on cognitive processing (e.g., MacIntyre & Gardner, 1994), language reception and interpretation (Horwitz et al., 1986), language attainment (e.g., Woodrow, 2006), willingness to use the TL or negligence of classroom duties (e.g., Horwitz et al., 1986; Piechurska-Kuciel, 2011b, 2014).

Conclusion

The aim of the present chapter was to shed light on the role of emotions in the process of L2 learning, particularly those that are the focus of the research project conducted for the purpose of this study. To this effect, the first section focused more generally on the role of positive (e.g., love and hope) and negative emotions (e.g., shame and guilt) in L2 teaching and learning in traditional settings and CALL. The following two sections narrowed the focus of attention to the emotions under investigation in the present study. Accordingly, Section 2 was dedicated to an overview of theoretical issues concerning the positive emotions of curiosity and enjoyment, presenting the definitions of these two emotions, their types and/or dimensions as well as sources. Section 3, in turn, was devoted to the negative emotions of boredom and anxiety. Following the structure of Section 2, the two constructs were discussed in the light of theories illuminating their definitions, typologies and sources. The four emotions may be experienced by language learners with varying degrees of intensity, and this experience may be influenced by a variety of causes. As such, the experience of different emotions may have a profound impact on L2 learning and teaching. This is inevitably connected with a student's decision whether or not to be active during language lessons and/or search for opportunities of L2 learning outside school. The following chapter will be devoted to an overview of empirical investigations of positive and negative emotions in L2 learning and teaching in traditional and CALL contexts.

2 Research on positive and negative emotions in L2 learning and teaching in conventional settings and CALL

Introduction

The present chapter is devoted to an overview of studies concerning the role of positive and negative emotions in second language (L2) learning and teaching in traditional settings and computer-assisted language learning (CALL). The empirical investigations reviewed also include those that have investigated temporal changes in levels of emotional states as well as factors accountable for such fluctuations. Importantly, the present discussion is confined to the emotions that are the focus of the study reported in Chapter 4. Accordingly, the first section provides an overview of state-of-the-art research on the positive emotions of curiosity and enjoyment and the negative emotions of anxiety and boredom in learning and teaching an L2 in traditional contexts. In a similar vein, the emphasis of the second section is also on these positive and negative emotions but this time in connection with cutting-edge studies concerning L2 learning and teaching in CALL settings. Due to the scarcity of empirical research related to the investigation of positive emotions in the realm of CALL, Section 2 mostly focuses on the discussion of the outcomes of research projects concerning the negative emotions of language anxiety and boredom, but it also includes an overview of the handful of studies regarding not only enjoyment but also curiosity and pride.

Research on positive and negative emotions in conventional settings

This section is devoted to a discussion of the most recent studies (conducted in 2014 or later) concerning the positive emotions of curiosity and enjoyment and the negative emotions of anxiety and boredom, especially in relation to changes in the levels of such emotions, as experienced by L2 learners in traditional contexts. These studies approached the four emotions from a variety of perspectives, involving, for example, the employment of different samples, the implementation of an array of data collection instruments and the use of diverse methods of data analysis. Moreover, such empirical investigations have often examined a given emotion in relation to other emotions and/or variables, different target languages and different time frames (e.g., they were

DOI: 10.4324/9781003240068-3

20 *Research on positive and negative emotions*

of cross-sectional or longitudinal design). What follows is a detailed description of these studies, which are presented in chronological order.

Dewaele and MacIntyre (2014)

The main aims of Dewaele and MacIntyre's (2014) study were to investigate levels of Foreign Language Enjoyment (FLE) and Foreign Language Classroom Anxiety (FLCA) in the language classroom, the link between these two emotions, as well as the effect of a number of factors (e.g., age, sex, languages known, number of languages studied, mastery of an L2, relative standing in the group or education level) on FLE and FLCA. The participants comprised an international cohort of language learners ($N = 1746$). The data were collected by means of a questionnaire that included a demographics section, 29 items concerning the two emotions, and an open-ended question that asked participants to provide a description of an enjoyable event in learning an L2. The quantitative findings revealed that levels of the positive emotion of enjoyment were significantly higher than the levels of the negative emotion of anxiety. Moreover, they appeared to be "independent emotions, and not opposite ends of the same dimension" (Dewaele & MacIntyre, 2014, p. 261). It was also found that the two emotions were connected to a host of variables, which included, among other things, the respondents' perception of their relative level of L2 proficiency in the classroom, number of languages known, the participants' age, and their education level. For example, older participants reported significantly more FLE and less FLCA. In addition, the analysis revealed that female learners experienced more enjoyment and more language anxiety than male students. It was also found that the cultural background of the respondents had a significant role to play with regard to the two emotions under study. Specifically, the Asian students reported the lowest levels of FLE and the highest levels of FLCA, while the North American learners exhibited the highest levels of FLE and the lowest levels of FLCA. Finally, the qualitative findings showed that enjoyment was triggered by teachers' professional and emotional skills, a supportive peer group, and moments at which participants realized that their effort in learning a foreign language paid off.

Kruk (2016b)

The objectives of Kruk's (2016b) quantitative study were to explore the changing character of boredom in an L2 classroom and its antecedents. The study involved 32 second- and fourth-grade male students learning English in secondary school, spanned a period of three weeks, and involved eight English lessons. The data were derived from two sets of research instruments. The first set was administered to the participants before the study got under way and included the Boredom Proneness Scale (BPS; Farmer & Sundberg, 1986) and the English Classroom Boredom Proneness Scale (ECBPS), which was a modified version of the BPS. More specifically, the ECBPS items were transformed into statements explicitly referring to the experience of the negative emotion of boredom in the L2 classroom. As regards the second set of data-gathering tools, it was employed during the lessons under investigation and encompassed five instruments: the English Classroom Boredom Grid (its aim was to measure the level of boredom indicated by the participants four times during a lesson on a seven-point scale), the Overall Assessment Scale (it required the learners to evaluate a lesson with respect to seven items on a semantic differential scale, such as interesting vs. boring, pleasant vs. unpleasant, monotonous vs. absorbing), class observations and teacher notes (these were used to describe the learners' behaviors without unduly interfering with the events they had been involved in), as well as lesson plans (they provided descriptions of the lessons with respect to their phases and language activities). The results showed that the experience of boredom during some lessons was in a state of flux, while in some others it remained relatively stable. The fluctuations in the experience of this aversive emotion were ascribed to such factors as, for example, the topics discussed, grammar exercises, the experience of being over-challenged and/or under-challenged, and the participants' overall susceptibility to boredom in the L2 classroom.

Kruk and Zawodniak (2017)

In their mixed-methods study, Kruk and Zawodniak (2017) investigated the relationship between general boredom susceptibility and boredom manifested in English classes, and the causes of this aversive emotion. The data-collection instruments included the Boredom Proneness Scale (Farmer & Sundberg, 1986), the Boredom in Practical English Language Classes Questionnaire (it consisted of 28 items related to boredom experienced in learning the L2) and a description of boredom-generating situations in the classroom. The data gathered via the instrument, completed by 174 English majors (125 females and 49 males), were subjected to quantitative and qualitative analysis. Quantitative analysis revealed a significant, positive correlation between overall boredom proneness and the experience of this emotion in English classes. In addition, boredom experienced in the classroom displayed a growing tendency with the passing of time (i.e., it was higher in the case of second- and third-year students when compared with their first-year counterparts). The qualitative analysis of the participants' descriptions related to the factors triggering the feelings of boredom yielded such causes of this negative emotion as repetitiveness and monotony of tasks, a mismatch between the level of challenge and the respondents' L2 proficiency, and the teacher, as well as modes of work imposed on the learners.

Dewaele and Dewaele (2017)

The pseudo-longitudinal study conducted by Dewaele and Dewaele (2017) aimed to compare changes in foreign language (FL) classroom enjoyment and

22 Research on positive and negative emotions

anxiety among three groups of language learners from two British secondary schools. More specifically, the sample consisted of a total of 189 subjects of different ages: 12–13, 14–15 and 16–18. The analysis of the data collected by means of a questionnaire showed that the emotions under investigation were relatively stable; however, enjoyment in L2 learning was predicted by different variables over time. In addition, the results revealed that, when compared to the middle age group (14–15), the feelings of anxiety and enjoyment in language learning in the youngest age group (12–13) and the oldest age group (16–18) were predicted by fewer learner-internal and teacher-centered variables. As for the middle age group, the emotions in question were predicted by attitude toward the FL, attitude toward the teacher, his or her (un)predictability and multilingualism. The results led the researchers to the conclusion that the constellation of factors related to the experience of emotions by the respondents evolved "at different speeds over time" (Dewaele & Dewaele, 2017, p. 20).

Kasbi and Elahi Shirvan (2017)

Kasbi and Elahi Shirvan (2017) focused on four Iranian intermediate-level female EFL learners' speaking anxiety from the perspective of Bronfenbrenner's (1979) ecosystem model and complex dynamic systems theory (CDST; Larsen-Freeman & Cameron, 2008). The qualitative analysis of the data gleaned from semi-structured interviews, non-participant classroom observation, and motometer indications (i.e., a drawing of a thermometer-shaped figure for measuring the level of anxiety every ten minutes on a 0–100 scale in five sessions) demonstrated that both internal and external factors influenced variation in the levels of anxiety experienced by the participants. To be more precise, fluctuations in the experience of this negative emotion were associated with three factors: (1) linguistic (e.g., the lack of vocabulary and/or grammar), (2) cognitive (e.g., the dearth of adequate knowledge regarding conversation topics) and (3) affective (e.g., assessment of teachers or peers, pressure, fear of negative evaluation and significant others). The findings also showed that changes in the participants' anxiety were induced by negative past experiences.

Boudreau, MacIntyre and Dewaele (2018)

The idiodynamic method (MacIntyre & Legatto, 2011), that is, a procedure that allows measurement of changes in the levels of an investigated variable on a moment-by-moment basis during the performance of a language task (e.g., a discussion), was used by Boudreau et al. (2018) to investigate the dynamics of anxiety and enjoyment in learning French as an L2. A group of ten Canadian English-speaking students with French as the target language were requested to perform two different communication tasks: storytelling (i.e., photograph description) and an oral interview (i.e., description, counting, giving directions and two discussions). During the performance of the language tasks the participants were equipped with ECG electrodes and they were also video recorded. Following the completion of the tasks, some students were requested to watch the videos and self-rate their levels of enjoyment while some other learners self-rated their levels of anxiety. In the follow-up interview, each student was presented with a graph that displayed his or her self-rated levels of the two emotions under study and asked to discuss factors that accounted for the changes. The obtained results showed that both emotions tended to fluctuate, often independently of each other, throughout the performance of the language tasks. The main reasons for these changes derived from the participants' interest and/or disinterest in the topic as well as some linguistic difficulties (e.g., lack of familiarity with suitable lexis).

Elahi Shirvan and Talebzadeh (2018)

In their study, Elahi Shirvan and Talebzadeh (2018) used a time-based sampling scheme of ecological momentary assessment (EMA) to explore the dynamism of various aspects of foreign language enjoyment across different timescales (e.g., minutes, weeks) throughout an English course. The participants were two female Iranian students. The data were collected at four levels. Level 1 involved the application of the idiodynamic method (MacIntyre & Legatto, 2011; see the previous study). Level 2 encompassed the use of an in-class enjoyment thermometer (i.e., a thermometer-shaped object drawn on a sheet of paper) in which the students were requested to rate their feeling of enjoyment on a scale ranging from 0 to 10 during a class every five minutes. Level 3 included weekly journal entries where the learners had the opportunity to reflect on their experience of enjoyment in L2 learning. Finally, at Level 4, a series of open-ended interviews were conducted at the start, middle and the end of the 16-week semester. The results showed that the positive emotion of enjoyment in learning an L2 fluctuated in terms of a hierarchy of temporal scales, from moment-to-moment variations to changes over months. Moreover, it was observed that each timescale contributed in a different way to the occurrence of enjoyment for each individual participant. Elahi Shirvan and Talebzadeh (2018) also found that "despite the dominance of some unique patterns of enjoyment for each individual at different timescales, the two participants experienced similar patterns of enjoyment under the influence of the same ecological factors" (p. 13).

Kruk (2018)

Kruk (2018) undertook a mixed-methods study whose aim was to investigate changes in foreign language anxiety levels as well as factors affecting such fluctuations. This longitudinal study included 52 Polish EFL secondary school students (aged 17–19), divided into four groups, and comprised 121 English lessons. The data were collected by means of an array of research instruments: the Foreign Language Classroom Anxiety Scale (FLCAS; Horwitz et al., 1986), a foreign language anxiety grid, an evaluation questionnaire, individual

24 *Research on positive and negative emotions*

interviews and lesson plans. While the administration of the FLCAS was intended to tap into changes in anxiety levels over a longer period of time (i.e., the scale was filled out three times throughout the semester), the purpose of the foreign language anxiety grid was to gauge the intensity of this negative emotion over a shorter timescale (i.e., the students self-rated their level of anxiety on a 1–7 scale four times during each lesson). As for the evaluation questionnaire, it contained four items on a semantic differential scale (e.g., relaxed vs. tense) and was completed toward the end of each lesson. When it comes to individual interviews and lesson plans, the former aimed at identifying factors responsible for changes in anxiety, while the latter offered details in this respect concerning particular lessons (e.g., their phases, language activities). The analysis of the data, gleaned from the research instruments described above, provided evidence for the dynamicity of this negative emotion concerning both the long- and short-term changes as well as factors accountable for their intensity. When it comes to the long-term changes, the experience of anxiety tended to reach its highest level at the beginning and the end of the school semester. It was also observed that some sequences of lessons were characterized by relatively stable levels in the experience of this emotion; however, such periods of stability were frequently preceded or followed by an unexpected rise or decline. As regards the short-term changes, on the whole, the highest level of anxiety was detected during the initial minutes of the lessons under investigation, while it was lowest at the end of each class. The qualitative findings revealed a number of factors responsible for these changes. Among other things, they included lack of confidence, speaking in the target language in front of peers, being called by the teacher, doing grammar exercises (especially those taken from the coursebooks) and completing tests.

Mahmoodzadeh and Khajavy (2019)

Mahmoodzadeh and Khajavy (2019) used Litman and Jimerson's (2004) model as a framework for conceptualizing language learning curiosity (LLC), which was designated as a separate variable anticipated to promote and maintain enjoyment, interest and willingness to learn a new language along with the already mastered L1. As a consequence, Mahmoodzadeh and Khajavy hypothesized LLC both as a feeling of interest and a feeling of deprivation. The former came into play while searching for means of using the L2 for communicative purposes and the latter was triggered while looking for opportunities of filling gaps in the knowledge of the L2. With this in mind, the researchers created and validated the Language Learning Curiosity Scale (LLCS) in their mixed-methods triangulation study carried out among 334 Iranian EFL learners. The results showed that while LLC was positively correlated with enjoyment and willingness to communicate, it was negatively associated with anxiety. It was also found that LLC is a socially situated positive emotion in the sense that it can be best developed through student-teacher and peer collaboration. Last but not least, it was revealed that creating a low-anxiety classroom environment was less significant than designing lessons and selecting language activities in arousing students' curiosity about learning an L2.

Liu and Xiangming (2019)

Liu and Xiangming (2019) conducted a longitudinal study whose aim was to uncover the dynamic character of the negative emotion of language anxiety and its effect on English language performance in a group of 324 first-year university students. In order to accomplish these goals, several research instruments were administered: the background questionnaire, English tests (which measured the participants' English language skills), the English Language Classroom Anxiety Scale (a modified version of the scale developed by Horwitz et al., 1986 and used in Liu, 2009), and the achievement anxiety test (to measure the extent to which test anxiety enhances student performance). The design of the study encompassed two phases. In the first stage (the beginning of the study), the participants completed a pre-test and a set of questionnaires. In the second phase (the end of the study), they took the post-test and again filled out the same set of questionnaires. Among other things, the results showed that at the end of the study the students turned out to be substantially less apprehensive of communication in English; they were less concerned about the English class or their performance in the TL. In addition, although the participants' general English language classroom anxiety was substantially lower, they proved to be more concerned about tests.

Kruk and Zawodniak (2020)

Kruk and Zawodniak (2020) comparatively examined 30 second-year English majors' feelings of the aversive emotion of boredom in learning English and German with respect to variations in its levels over the course of three semesters, as well as the causes of such fluctuations. The data were gathered by means of the Language Learning Boredom in Retrospect (LLBR) questionnaire in which the participants were requested to look back upon their experience of boredom in learning the languages in question. More specifically, the respondents were asked to reflect on their feelings regarding this negative emotion during the first, second and third semester at three different points in time, that is, at the start, middle and the end of each semester. In addition, the students were requested to self-rate the intensity of the experience of boredom during the three semesters on a seven-point scale (1 – lowest, 7 – highest). The analysis of the data revealed that for both languages the levels of boredom were the lowest at the start and the highest at the end of every semester. According to the researchers, this finding indicated that at the outset the participants apparently had high expectations and needs, which, however, may not have been properly provided for by the teachers as the course progressed. As for the changes in boredom levels detected from one semester to the next, the analysis uncovered some differences in learning English and German. While in the former case the participants experienced

26 *Research on positive and negative emotions*

the least and the most boredom in the first and the second semester, respectively, in the latter case, this aversive emotion was lowest in the first semester and reached its climax in the third semester. When it comes to the sources of boredom in learning English, they were grouped into three thematic categories: lesson-related (i.e., repeatability, uselessness and uninvolving language material, predictability of lessons/tasks and the level of difficulty), teacher-related (i.e., the way of conducting lessons, teaching methods/techniques, personal and/or physical characteristics of teachers) and other (i.e., class time, the weather and overall work overload). As for the causes of boredom in learning German, they involved four categories: lesson-related factors (e.g., similar lessons, uninteresting topics, repeatability of language material, the level of difficulty of tasks), reluctance to learn German, people-related factors (i.e., demanding teachers, teaching methods and techniques, and peers), as well as other causes (i.e., class time).

Pawlak, Kruk and Zawodniak (2020a)

The aims of a mixed-methods study carried out by Pawlak et al. (2020a) were to explore the patterns of boredom experienced in a single English class by 11 Polish university students majoring in English characterized by moderate (MBS) and high (HBS) levels of the negative emotion of boredom, and to find out whether those patterns were displayed in the individual students' trajectories of the emotion in question. Moreover, the researchers set out to uncover factors accountable for those trajectories. The data were gleaned from a number of research instruments: a background questionnaire, the Boredom in Practical English Language Classes Questionnaire (a modified version of an instrument developed by Kruk and Zawodniak, 2017) and an in-class boredom questionnaire. The last tool consisted of three main parts: a self-report boredom grid (i.e., a scale from 1 [minimum] to 7 [maximum] in which the students self-rated the level of boredom at five-minute intervals), an evaluation of the class based on a semantic differential scale, and a short narrative (i.e., a short description of the experience of boredom during the class). The analysis of the data led the researchers to conclude that general proneness to boredom in English classes was associated with the participants' unique patterns of this negative emotion. More specifically, the self-reported boredom levels were observed to change for both groups of students; however, some divergences were found between the two groups as well. The MBS group displayed a continuing increase in the intensity of the feeling of boredom and the HBS group showed a high level of this negative emotion during the entire class. Pawlak et al. (2020a) also uncovered the presence of discrepancies between general patterns of boredom and individual student trajectories in this respect. For instance, one member of the MBS group was more bored for most of the class than was indicated by the whole group's general disposition to experience boredom, and one learner in the HBS group was observed to display a much more diverse pattern of boredom than the majority of this

Research on positive and negative emotions 27

group. As for the factors responsible for shaping the intensity of boredom, the inspection of individual trajectories allowed the researchers to uncover constellations of factors and nuanced explanations of boredom triggers related to individual learners. These factors included, for example, the participants' self-awareness, learning experience or learning styles.

Pawlak, Kruk, Zawodniak and Pasikowski (2020b)

The quantitative study conducted by Pawlak et al. (2020b) was intended to identify factors underlying the experience of boredom in the L2 classroom, to uncover the mediating effects of general boredom proneness and attainment, and, ultimately, to design a research instrument that can be utilized to tap into this aversive emotion among advanced language learners. The participants were 107 English majors (80 females and 27 males) who completed the Boredom Proneness Scale (Farmer & Sundberg, 1986) and the Boredom in Practical English Language Classes (BPELC) questionnaire. The items contained within these two instruments, together with the respondents' end-of-the-year examination grades, allowed the researchers to group the participants into less and more prone to boredom as well as high and low achievers. Exploratory factor analysis and independent samples *t*-tests allowed distinguishing two factors underlying boredom, that is, (F1) disengagement, monotony and repetitiveness, and (F2) lack of satisfaction and challenge. These two factors were linked with two essential facets of boredom experienced in English classes, namely, reactive and proactive. The former was related to calibrating, indifferent and apathetic boredom and the latter concerned searching boredom. Moreover, the analysis showed that the participants who were generally more prone to boredom were also statistically significantly more likely to succumb to the feelings of this negative emotion in English classes, and this tendency was manifested for both factors. It was also found that low achievers were statistically significantly more likely to exhibit boredom than high achievers regarding F1; however, in the case of F2, the difference between the two groups of students failed to reach significance. According to the researchers, this finding may have been an indication of more successful students' greater likelihood to endure in unengaging, uninteresting and insufficiently inspiring language activities, which may be due to their better understanding of the fact that attaining learning goals comes at the expense of doing things that may be innately less appealing. However, Pawlak et al. (2020b) also suggest that the apparent lack of satisfaction and challenge may be less linked to attainment in view of the fact that both more and less successful students may be eager to get out of the vicious circle of performing boring language tasks and sticking to related routines, provided that, for example, very appealing activities are offered by their teachers. Perhaps most importantly, the analysis of the data led to the development of the Boredom in Practical English Language Classes – Revised (BPELC-R), a new data-collection instrument.

28 *Research on positive and negative emotions*

Pawlak, Zawodniak and Kruk (2020c)

In this mixed-methods study, Pawlak et al. (2020c) examined differences in the levels of boredom and factors accountable for them in the case of 23 third-year students of English at university level, divided into two groups (one including 13 students and the other 10 learners), during four integrated skills classes. Apart from this, the researchers sought to identify differences in the experience of boredom among individual participants and factors responsible for this negative emotion. The data were gathered with the help of a set of research instruments, similar to those used in the study carried out by Pawlak et al. (2020a) described earlier: a background questionnaire (to provide demographic information regarding the students), a semi-structured interview (to obtain additional information on the nature of boredom and its changes), lesson plans with annotations (used to provide detailed information concerning the conducted classes) and an in-class boredom questionnaire. The in-class boredom questionnaire constituted the main research instrument and it consisted of four parts. Part One included information about a given participant. Part Two contained a boredom grid in which the participants were requested to self-rate their level of boredom on a scale ranging from 1 (minimum) to 7 (maximum) at five-minute intervals. Part Three required the students to evaluate each class with respect to seven items on a semantic differential scale (e.g., dull vs. exciting, unsatisfying vs. satisfying, monotonous vs. absorbing), which was subsequently converted into a seven-point Likert scale. Finally, Part Four requested the participants to write a short narrative about their experience of boredom during each class. The analysis of the data revealed, among other things, that the negative emotion of boredom was subject to changes within a single language activity, an entire class and from one class to another. These fluctuations were ascribed to the nature of the activity in hand, monotony and repetitiveness, the opportunity to interact with peers, the phase of the class, or some individual characteristics and dispositions. It was also found that the trajectories of boredom displayed by individual participants often considerably diverged from patterns recorded for entire groups and they were influenced differently by a number of internal and external variables that were subject to alteration over time.

Dewaele and Dewaele (2020)

Dewaele and Dewaele (2020) set out to investigate the effect of the language teacher on positive and negative emotions, that is, foreign language enjoyment and foreign language anxiety, or, in more specific terms, the experience of the said emotions in the same language taught by two different L2 teachers. The study involved 40 high school learners who studied modern languages with one main and one secondary teacher. The analysis of the data obtained from the online questionnaire involving items related to the participants' demographic information, their learning of an L2, foreign language enjoyment and foreign language anxiety showed that the feeling of enjoyment was significantly higher with the main teacher, whereas the experience of anxiety remained similar with both teachers. Moreover, the predictors of the positive emotion of enjoyment, that is, attitudes toward the teacher, frequency of use of the L2 by the teacher during a lesson and unpredictability, turned out to be significantly more positive for the participants' main teacher. It was also found that the teacher generating a positive emotional atmosphere in the classroom contributed to higher feelings of enjoyment. Finally, the findings demonstrated that pride, attitudes toward learning a foreign language and group membership as well as the peers, or, in other words, items that reflected more stable personal and group characteristics, were less likely to vary between the two teachers. The findings suggest that foreign language enjoyment may be more teacher-dependent, whereas language anxiety is more stable across teachers.

Elahi Shirvan and Taherian (2021)

The aims of the longitudinal study carried out by Elahi Shirvan and Taherian (2021) were to investigate the growth and changing trends of the positive emotion of enjoyment and the negative emotion of anxiety among a group of university students by means of latent growth curve modeling (LGCM), as well as a methodological triangulation in the form of reliance on different data collection tools. The participants were 367 undergraduate students (aged 18–25) who attended a course of general English over a period of one semester. The data were collected with the help of the following research instruments: the Foreign Language Enjoyment Scale (FLE; Dewaele & MacIntyre, 2014), eight items adapted from the Foreign Language Classroom Anxiety Scale (Horwitz et al., 1986), written journals, semi-structured interviews and observations. The quantitative analysis of the data uncovered an increase in the participants' experience of enjoyment and a decrease in their feeling of the negative emotion of anxiety throughout the semester. Moreover, the initial levels of both emotions could not predict their growth throughout the semester. It was also found that at the start of the semester, the significant negative correlation between the participants' experience of the two emotions in question was low but in the course of the semester the strength of this relationship tended to grow. The qualitative findings revealed, however, that the students simultaneously experienced moments of both low and high levels of the two emotions under investigation.

Li, Huang and Li (2021)

The study conducted by Li et al. (2021) sought to examine the joint effects of trait emotional intelligence and classroom environment on enjoyment and anxiety in L2 learning. A total of 3,013 students participated in the study, 1,718 of whom were secondary learners and 1,295 university students. The data were collected by means of four scales dealing with classroom environment, trait emotional intelligence, foreign language enjoyment and foreign language anxiety, and subjected to correlation and regression analyses. The

30 *Research on positive and negative emotions*

results showed that trait emotional intelligence and classroom environment significantly predicted enjoyment and anxiety in learning a foreign language, both separately and jointly. It was also found that while the negative emotion of anxiety in L2 learning was predicted more strongly by trait emotional intelligence and less by classroom environment, the positive emotion of enjoyment was to a lesser extent predicted by trait emotional intelligence and more by classroom environment. Based on the findings, the researchers suggested two main implications. The first relates to the improvement of the classroom environment, which has the potential to foster language learners' classroom emotions, whereas the second concerns the need for training in teacher and learner trait emotional intelligence.

Kruk, Pawlak and Zawodniak (2021)

Kruk et al.'s (2021) mixed-methods study was undertaken to investigate changes in the levels of boredom experienced by a group of 13 English majors in four EFL classes, as well as factors contributing to such fluctuations. The data collection instruments included a background questionnaire, an in-class boredom questionnaire, a semi-structured interview, and lesson plans. The background questionnaire supplied information related to the participants, the semi-structured interviews were utilized to obtain a better understanding of the participants' feelings related to the negative emotion in question during each class, and the lesson plans offered information concerning the classes, their phases and tasks performed by the students. Like the study conducted by Pawlak et al. (2020a) described earlier, the in-class boredom questionnaire consisted of several parts. The first part elicited information regarding the participants. The second part encompassed a boredom grid in which the students self-rated the level of their boredom on a scale from 1 (minimum) to 7 (maximum) at five-minute intervals. The third part included a semantic differential scale, which was used by the learners to assess each class. The fourth part asked the students to write a short paragraph about their experience of boredom during each class. The data collected by means of the discussed instruments were subjected to a combination of quantitative and qualitative analysis. The results demonstrated that the intensity of boredom was subject to major variations over different timescales. More specifically, this negative emotion fluctuated from one class to the next as well as within each class; however, the scope and amplitude of such changes varied. It was also uncovered that even though this aversive emotion turned out to be ascribed to a distinct constellations of factors, it was largely attributable to repetitiveness, monotony and predictability of what transpired during a specific class.

Nakamura, Darasawang and Reinders (2021)

The study conducted by Nakamura et al. (2021) was intended to investigate the antecedents of the negative emotion of boredom in a group of 25 second-year Thai university students enrolled in an English oral communication course. The data were collected with the help of an online questionnaire and focus group interviews. The purpose of the questionnaire was to elicit the participants' experiences of boredom in a given class over the course of seven weeks. The interview aimed at obtaining in-depth insights into the feelings of boredom and its antecedents in the L2 learning context, as well as the students' experiences of boredom in the classroom. Constant comparative analysis of the data gathered through the questionnaire generated nine thematic factors as the antecedents of boredom, which were further corroborated by the interview findings. The nine factors were (1) unfavorable appraisals of the task (e.g., uninteresting, unimportant or too easy), (2) activity mismatch (i.e., negative perceptions of a given situation), (3) lack of comprehension concerning, for example, the content and TL features presented in the textbook, teachers' explanations or task requirements, (4) physical fatigue (e.g., tiredness and sleepiness usually due to lack of sleep), (5) insufficient L2 knowledge (e.g., deficiencies in L2 skills that impacted task performance), (6) task difficulty (e.g., a debate), (7) negative behaviors of classmates (e.g., disruptiveness or lack of engagement), (8) lack of ideas (i.e., inadequate content to share in a given task) and (9) input overload (e.g., the learners' perception of receiving too much input while reading long passages of text).

Li (2021)

In her mixed-methods study, Li (2021) drew on the control-value theory (CVT) of achievement emotions (Pekrun, 2006; Pekrun et al., 2010) to examine control-value appraisals as antecedents of boredom in learning English as a foreign language. The participants were 2,002 Chinese university students who completed a composite questionnaire focusing on control appraisal, value appraisals and measures of boredom in learning English as a foreign language. The items included in the questionnaire were taken from existing instruments such as, for example, Marsh (1992), Frenzel et al. (2007) and Pekrun et al. (2011), and modified accordingly. In addition, 11 students and 11 English teachers took part in a subsequent interview. Using Pearson correlation analyses and regression analyses, Li demonstrated that different control-value appraisals predicted boredom uniquely or interactively. More specifically, perceived control and value negatively predicted boredom since, overall, the learners who felt more competent in learning the English language or who valued it more had a tendency to feel less bored and vice versa. The qualitative results supported and expanded upon the quantitative results by uncovering more complexities in the relationships between control-value appraisals and boredom. It was found that the individuals experienced boredom when they had the feeling of being overwhelmingly challenged or under-challenged in learning the target language, indicating the possible existence of upper and lower boundaries for the negative influences of control-value appraisals on boredom.

32 *Research on positive and negative emotions*

Li, Dewaele and Hu (2021)

Li et al. (2021) conducted a two-step investigation of foreign language learning boredom with regard to Chinese university non-English-major EFL students and English teachers. The goals of their first study were to present evidence on the occurrence of boredom among Chinese university non-English-major EFL learners from both the learners' and the teachers' perspectives, as well as to offer an empirical foundation for the conceptualization of the construct of foreign language learning boredom (FLLB). In order to accomplish these goals, the researchers interviewed 22 students and 11 English language teachers. In addition, 659 students filled out an online questionnaire in which they were requested to recall and describe their perceptions and experiences concerning the experience of the negative emotion of boredom in learning the English language. The analysis of the collected data showed that boredom was a frequently experienced negative emotion among the participants. Additionally, the gathered data allowed a basis for offering a multidimensional conceptualization of boredom in foreign language learning as a construct "characterized by negative valence, low arousal and being achievement-related activity-focused" (p. 22). Regarding the antecedents of FLLB, Li et al. (2021) found that the negative emotion in question occurred when an ongoing language activity was recognized as over- or under-challenging. The aims of the second study were to develop and validate the measure of boredom in the context of the research project. With the help of 808 and 2,223 respondents in the pilot and the main study, respectively, the researchers developed the Foreign Language Learning Boredom Scale (FLLBS), which, among other things, encompassed the social dimension of boredom related to learner-internal and learner-external facets (peers, teachers, learning tasks and materials) and was intended for non-English-major EFL learners.

Jin, Dewaele and MacIntyre (2021)

Jin et al. (2021) set out to experimentally examine whether the participants' reminiscences about foreign language proficiency development efficiently lessened their experience of the negative emotion of language anxiety in the classroom. In addition, the researchers investigated the learners' recollections concerning their proficiency development and the types of evoked emotions. The participants were 88 Chinese university students majoring in English, who were randomly assigned to two groups: experimental ($N = 43$) and control ($N = 45$). All the students were requested to complete an English classroom anxiety scale based on Jin and Dewaele (2018) before and after a 30-day intervention. Moreover, throughout the experimental period the members of the experimental group completed reminiscing tasks and they were asked to describe their emotional experiences in each recollecting performance.

Research on positive and negative emotions 33

The quantitative analysis of the data gleaned from the questionnaire administered before and after the intervention demonstrated that the negative emotion under study was significantly reduced over time at the overall and dimensional (i. e., fear and worry) levels in the experimental group but it remained stable in the control group. The qualitative analysis of the gathered data uncovered three aspects the students in the experimental group reminisced about: (1) progress in the development of English proficiency, (2) non-language proficiency progress and (3) emotions. As for the first aspect, the learners, in particular, recalled their progress in the four language skills (i.e., speaking, listening, writing, reading) and the TL subsystems (i.e., vocabulary, grammar and pronunciation). As regards the second aspect, the students most frequently recalled their progress in cross-cultural knowledge about English-speaking countries, testing, learning ability (e. g., knowledge of learning theories and approaches, memorization, self-directed learning) and psychological resources (e.g., confidence, interest and enjoyment). Finally, the emotion aspect was related to positive and negative emotions, with the former being more frequently recalled than the latter. The top prominent positive emotions included happiness, confidence, contentment, sense of accomplishment, pride and enjoyment, whereas the major negative ones were sadness, restlessness, anxiety, confusion, nervousness, fear and distress.

Research on positive and negative emotions in CALL settings

This section is dedicated to an overview of state-of-the-art research projects related to positive and negative emotions, particularly with regard to changes in their levels, experienced by language learners in the context of CALL. These empirical investigations, which are evidently few in number, mostly concern the negative emotions of language anxiety and boredom but also include some studies focusing on the positive emotions of enjoyment, curiosity and pride. As was the case with the previous section, they are presented and discussed in chronological order.

Lai, Zhu and Gong (2015)

The main goal of the study conducted by Lai et al. (2015) was to survey 82 Chinese EFL secondary school learners on their out-of-class English language learning in order to unravel the characteristics of the experiences linked to good learning outcomes. The requisite data were collected via a questionnaire and an interview with selected participants. Among other things, Lai and colleagues found that the respondents' use of technology outside the classroom was positively and significantly associated with enjoyment in learning the target language. In addition, the qualitative data revealed that learners with a higher sense of L2 enjoyment engaged in a number of technology-based activities, which included such tasks as, for example, watching English movies, listening to English songs and communicating in English via microblog.

34   *Research on positive and negative emotions*

Kruk (2016a)

Kruk's (2016a) study, which used a combination of quantitative and qualitative methodologies and spanned a period of one semester, aimed to investigate fluctuations in the levels of the negative emotions of boredom and anxiety (along with motivation) experienced by a group of 16 female English majors while visiting the virtual world Second Life (SL) and to identify the main influences on the observed changes. The requisite data were gathered by means of the session log completed by the participants before, during and after each visit to SL. The tool comprised three parts. The first part, filled out by the students before each visit, asked for their name, session date, its topic and aim. The second part included three grids, where the participants were requested to self-rate their levels of boredom, anxiety and motivation at five-minute intervals on a seven-point scale (1 – minimum, 7 – maximum). They were also asked to indicate the amount of time spent in SL during each session. Regarding the third part of the instrument, it required the participants to briefly describe each visit to SL (e.g., their activities in SL, learning benefits, reflections). The analysis of the self-ratings uncovered dynamically changing levels of boredom and motivation but relatively stable levels of language anxiety. More specifically, the levels of boredom had a tendency to increase over time, but the levels of motivation showed a decreasing trend. With regard to the factors accountable for the decrease in boredom levels, they encompassed the participants' willingness to use SL as a tool allowing them to practice English with enjoyment while communicating with SL users, explore the virtual environment, have the freedom to select a topic for conversation or autonomously set goals for each session. As for the explanations for the increases in the self-reported levels of boredom, they included reluctance to get involved in conversations exhibited by some SL residents, meeting impolite or unfriendly users, difficulties with being understood by others, unanticipated termination of conversations and some technical issues. When it comes to the participants' occasional experiences of language anxiety, they occurred when meeting rude and aggressive SL users as well as SL residents who asked inappropriate questions.

Kruk (2016c)

The aim of the study conducted by Kruk (2016c) was to investigate the levels of the negative emotion of language anxiety experienced by 27 high school students in the virtual world *Yoowalk*. The students were divided into two groups and asked to perform online language activities (both on the internet and in the virtual world *Yoowalk* – Group 1) and conventional language activities in the language classroom (Group 2). Quantitative analysis of the data collected through the Foreign Language Classroom Anxiety Scale (Horwitz et al., 1986) before and after the instructional treatment showed that the use of the online environment had a slightly greater effect on reducing the level of the negative emotion under investigation in students in Group 1 compared to those in Group 2. This said, the most positive impact of the virtual environment was revealed in the case of communication apprehension, the lower level of which was observed immediately after the lessons.

Melchor-Couto (2017)

The aim of Melchor-Couto's (2017) mixed-methods study was to investigate the evolution of foreign language anxiety experienced by seven language learners who interacted orally in four sessions in the virtual environment of SL when compared with a group of seven students who conducted similar oral tasks in dyads during four language lessons held in the traditional classroom. The data were collected through a set of questionnaires and were subsequently subjected to quantitative and qualitative analysis. The findings showed that the students who performed oral tasks in SL displayed a decrease in the intensity of anxiety over time and they felt less anxious when compared with their traditional counterparts (i.e., the students who performed the oral tasks in conventional settings). On the whole, Melchor-Couto (2017) attributed the decline in the experience of this negative emotion to the participants' heightened confidence during oral interactions in SL as well as the anonymity provided by the virtual environment.

Zawodniak and Kruk (2018b)

In another study, involving a sample of four female participants taken from the research project conducted by Kruk (2016a), Zawodniak and Kruk (2018b) explored the influence of the students' visits to the virtual world SL on changes in levels of the negative emotions of boredom and anxiety (alongside motivation) as well as the main causes accounting for these fluctuations. The main research instruments used to collect data were (1) a three-part session log (for details see the description above: Kruk, 2016a) and (2) an evaluation questionnaire, which required the participants to indicate the influence of SL on their experience of boredom and anxiety as well as the levels of motivation. In the case of boredom, a percentage scale was used and in the case of the other two constructs, a seven-point scale (1 – minimum, 7 – maximum) was employed. The results revealed the dynamic character of all the variables under investigation; however, their intensity and amplitude differed for the individual learners. These changes were also found to interact with an array of factors. In the case of boredom, these factors included the students' expectations, the unwillingness of SL users to interact in English, the time of session, difficulty in finding meaning in what the participants were doing, and the lack of skills needed for specific activities characteristic of this virtual environment (e.g., shopping). As for the changes in the experience of language anxiety, they concerned, on the one hand, the occasional lack of opportunity to communicate in the TL, and, on the other hand, the interaction with more proficient speakers or their unwillingness to communicate in English.

36 *Research on positive and negative emotions*

Elahi Shirvan and Taherian (2018)

The main aim of the longitudinal study carried out by Elahi Shirvan and Taherian (2018) was to explore variations in the experience of the negative emotion of anxiety of four EFL learners throughout a virtual language course through a complexity lens in accordance with the core assumptions of complex dynamic systems theory (i.e., changeability, variability and context dependence; cf. e.g., Larsen-Freeman, 2016). The experience of this negative emotion during language activities performed by the participants in the learning environment in question was determined by means of two research instruments, namely, a motometer and a learning journal. The former instrument took the form of a thermometer-shaped figure drawn on a sheet of paper with a scale ranging from 0 (minimum anxiety) to 100 (maximum anxiety). The participants marked their anxiety every ten minutes within an 80-minute online session, which allowed the researchers to measure the changing levels in the intensity of anxiety. The latter tool was utilized to gain greater insights regarding the learners' feelings with respect to anxiety during each session. The analysis uncovered changes in the levels of anxiety throughout the virtual course as well as stable patterns of this negative emotion. Moreover, the findings revealed the importance of the learning context and its contribution to changes in learners' anxiety. According to Elahi Shirvan and Taherian (2018, p. 431), "taking a range of potentially interconnected elements into consideration, sometimes a specific situation can cause a change in students' anxiety. However, in some cases no clear explanation can be offered. Hence, we propose that through the meticulous lens of the dynamic system theory, we can appropriately investigate the process of learning."

Kruk (2019)

The focus of the mixed-methods study conducted by Kruk (2019) over a span of one semester in the context of the virtual world SL was guided by three aims: (1) to investigate two English majors' (one male and one female) boredom and language anxiety (together with willingness to communicate and motivation) during a single visit to the virtual environment in question as well as from one visit to the next, (2) to uncover the relationship among these variables, and (3) to reveal possible influences on the variations that these variables underwent. As in the research projects described above (i.e., Kruk, 2016a; Zawodniak & Kruk, 2018b), the data were collected by means of a three-part session log and they were analyzed quantitatively and qualitatively. The findings showed that all the constructs under investigation were subject to change both during a single session in SL as well as from one visit to another, with the caveat that the degree of these changes varied depending on the learner. It was also revealed that the individual trajectories of the experienced emotions deviated from the overall, averaged trajectory of each variable. Moreover, the results showed that the variables, including the negative emotions of boredom and language anxiety, interacted in a dynamic and unpredictable manner; however, convergent trends could also be observed (e.g., trajectories of boredom and language anxiety from one visit to another). Similarly to previous studies, factors influencing the dynamics of the investigated emotions turned out to be, for example, interesting topics, comprehending information provided by interlocutors, meeting unpleasant users, monotony, or prior experiences.

Lee and Hsieh (2019)

In their quantitative study, conducted among 261 Taiwanese EFL undergraduate students, Lee and Hsieh (2019) investigated the relationship between a set of affective variables (i.e., self-confidence, language anxiety, motivation and grit) and willingness to communicate (WTC) in three communicative contexts (i.e., inside and outside the classroom as well as digital). The analysis of the data obtained through a questionnaire revealed that the participants who were characterized by higher levels of grit and confidence in learning an L2 manifested higher WTC in L2 in all settings under investigation (i.e., in and out of class as well as digital). Such results, according to Lee and Hsieh, suggested that language learners who were confident about communicating in the TL, as well as persistent in learning and using this language in spite of the encountered obstacles, had a tendency to initiate communication in English in both digital and offline environments. Importantly, the results also showed that the lack of language anxiety turned out to be a significant predictor of the respondents' WTC in non-digital settings (i.e., in- and out-of-class contexts) but not in the digital environment. Based on the findings, the researchers concluded that contemporary L2 learners might feel more relaxed with communicating in an L2 by means of digital technology than through traditional means. Lee and Hsieh (2019) also suggested that digital settings offer social support and further psychological advantages, which possibly contribute to generating a less anxiety-evoking milieu for language learners.

Yoshida (2020a)

The aim of Yoshida's (2020a) study was to explore positive and negative emotions during online text chats as well as factors accountable for these emotions. The research project involved 15 learners of Japanese who participated in seven online text chats carried out in the TL with native Japanese speakers over a period of seven weeks. The data were collected by means of a set of research instruments that included questionnaires concerning the participants' demographic information and their prior experiences related to text chats, the students' written reports regarding their chats, transcripts of the chats, as well as questions that emerged from e-mail exchanges between the participants and the researcher whose aim was to clarify specific issues included in the reports. The analysis showed a host of both positive and negative emotions that came to the

38 *Research on positive and negative emotions*

fore in the course of online text chats. While the most regularly evoked positive emotion turned out to be the feeling of enjoyment, the feeling of difficulty proved to be the most frequent negative emotion. In addition, the findings demonstrated that both positive and negative emotions tended to change over time (i.e., across seven weeks). As far as the causes of the revealed emotions are concerned, the positive ones were elicited by interlocutors and conversations involving common interests and culture, whereas the negative emotions were generated by issues with the Japanese language and the chat process. As pointed out by Yoshida (2020a), in order to boost L2 learners' positive emotions in online text exchanges, which may result in learning gains, it is vital for students to develop a good rapport with their interlocutors and to shy away from paying too much attention to their own foreign language ability.

Yoshida (2020b)

The main goals of the study conducted by Yoshida (2020b) were to determine the types of emotional scaffolding offered by Japanese-speaking students in Japanese text chats with learners of Japanese as an L2 as well as to find out what positive emotions those learners experienced as a consequence of the emotional scaffolding. The data were gathered from a group of 19 students who attended a third-year (intermediate) course in Japanese at an Australian university and who, for the purpose of the chat project, were paired with Japanese students learning English at a Japanese university. The data, gathered with the help of weekly reports, chat transcripts and interviews, showed that emotional scaffolding found in the data encompassed features such as the expression of positive attitudes toward the chat itself and expressions signifying shared feelings, specifically about the text chats and learning the TL. Moreover, the emotional scaffolding included complimenting of the participant's language abilities, the expressions of emotions by means of emoticons and other symbols, as well as the use of casual forms (e.g., expressions of friendliness). The analysis of the data also revealed that text chats that lacked emotional scaffolding were structured like interviews. More specifically, they contained polite expressions that indicated distance between the chatters, they lacked emotional expressions and expressions of friendliness. It was also uncovered that text chats with emotional scaffolding tended to generate positive emotions in the participants. These included the feelings of enjoyment, fun, comfort, confidence and motivation. By contrast, text chats that lacked emotional scaffolding led to the emergence of negative emotions (i.e., boredom and the feelings of awkwardness) among the students.

Hong, Hwang, Liu and Tai (2020)

According to Hong et al. (2020), various types of gamification can be beneficial to improving L2 learning. Keeping this in mind, Hong et al. concentrated on the gamifying of learning content by language learners in order to confirm the

Research on positive and negative emotions 39

effectiveness of gamification as a learning activity and to explore the effects of students posing and gamifying questions in connection with learning L2 grammar. The researchers utilized a gamification platform (TipOn) to enable the learners to create and gamify questions depending on the different game modes to help their peers practice English grammar. More specifically, the learners ($N = 96$) were requested to pose and gamify questions concerning TL grammar using the said platform. In addition, Hong et al. set out to uncover emotional regulation effects of posing and gamifying questions on TL performance by investigating how the participants' two types of epistemic curiosity, that is, interest-type epistemic curiosity and deprivation-type epistemic curiosity, influenced their attitude toward gamification and their learning progress. The analysis of the data revealed that the experience of foreign language anxiety was negatively related to the two types of epistemic curiosity. The findings also showed that although the interest-type epistemic curiosity did not have any significant impact on the learners' attitude toward gamification, the deprivation-type epistemic curiosity was positively associated with the students' attitude toward gamification. Last but not least, the results demonstrated that attitudes toward gamification positively predicted the participants' progress in L2 learning. Based on the results, Hong et al. (2020) suggested that teachers should use a gamifying system in a flipped classroom to encourage language learners to tap into their epistemic curiosity to enhance their learning content and language learning in general.

Li and Dewaele (2020)

Drawing on Pekrun's (2006) control-value theory, Li and Dewaele's (2020) study investigated the predictive effects of trait emotional intelligence (TEI) and online learning achievement perceptions on the negative emotion of boredom experienced during an online English course. The participants were 348 Chinese tertiary students who were asked to complete an online composite questionnaire, which consisted of four parts regarding the participants' background information, the Trait Emotional Intelligence Questionnaire – Short Form (Petrides, 2009), the Online Learning Achievement Perception Scale, and the Foreign Language Classroom Boredom Subscale. Quantitative analysis demonstrated that the respondents manifested a medium level of TEI and moderate perceptions of online learning gains. Moreover, the learners exhibited a low to medium level of boredom, which, however, was significantly higher in comparison with the traditional face-to-face English classes. The researchers also found that TEI and achievement perceptions negatively co-predicted the experience of boredom. More specifically, the former showed a small to medium effect and the latter revealed a medium to large effect. The findings confirmed the relevance of the control-value theory in online foreign language teaching.

40 *Research on positive and negative emotions*

Bashori, van Hout, Strik and Cucchiarini (2020)

Bashori et al. (2020) investigated the occurrence of foreign language speaking anxiety (FLSA) among 573 Indonesian EFL high school learners in a web-based language learning environment. In particular, the study set out to explore the impact of two Automatic Speech Recognition (ASR-based) learning websites (i.e., www.iloveindonesia.my.id and NovoLearning) on the participants' speaking anxiety. The data collection instruments included a set of questionnaires and interviews tapping into the experience of anxiety. The findings revealed that, on the whole, the participants showed a moderate to serious level of FLSA, the more anxious and less anxious students assessed web-based language learning positively, and they were of the opinion that this learning environment could lessen their speaking anxiety. Of particular significance was the finding that the participants' experience of this negative emotion was lower when speaking in the target language within the context of ASR-based websites in comparison to speaking to peers or other individuals.

Sampson and Yoshida (2020)

The study conducted by Sampson and Yoshida (2020) focused on two undergraduate students (taken from a larger group of participants) from Japan and Australia, Shota and Michelle, in order to obtain deeper insights into their dynamic perceptions of feelings linked with communicative interactions during seven chat sessions conducted via the messaging application LINE. The data were collected by means of a reflective session report in which the participants were requested to describe each chat. The tool included open-ended prompts that asked them about their feelings during communication, their perceptions of communication skills, linguistic and cultural aspects, as well as aspects regarding positive or negative elements in the chats. The obtained results demonstrated that regardless of taking part in the same dyad during the chats, Shota indicated a lot more unpleasant feelings (e.g., anxiety and feeling disappointed), while Michelle reported far more pleasant feelings (e.g., enjoyment, the sense of interest and achievement/progress). Based on their findings, Sampson and Yoshida drew attention to the importance of situated, dynamic and socially aware research into the complexity of emotions inevitably related to L2 learning.

Kruk (2021a)

The study conducted by Kruk (2021a) was undertaken with two aims in mind: (1) to explore one English female's changes in boredom levels during single visits to SL and from one session to another, and (2) to identify the factors causing them. The data were gathered through a number of research instruments, which included a background questionnaire, the Learning Style

Survey (Cohen et al., 2002), a session log and a semi-structured interview. As for the background questionnaire, it contained demographic information concerning the participant. The session log resembled the design of the instrument utilized in previous studies conducted by the researcher (i.e., Kruk, 2016a, 2019). The semi-structured interview was conducted with the student after the last session in SL and its open-ended format was to prompt the interviewee to ruminate on her own emotions and behaviors in a reflective and exploratory manner in order to shed more light on the issue under investigation. The results showed that the experience of boredom in the context of a virtual world can be dynamic (i.e., it may be subject to fluctuations in the intensity of its experience during individual sessions as well as from one session to another). The analysis also showed that changes in the levels of boredom can be caused, for example, by meeting the same interlocutors, shortage of discussion topics, monotonous conversations, group discussions, interactions that do not contribute to linguistic development or encountering rude or aggressive users. Despite the fact that some of the findings were in line with the results of previous studies pertaining to boredom in L2 learning (e.g., Chapman, 2013; Kruk, 2016b), focusing on just one individual allowed the researcher to yield new insights into the emotion under investigation. This is because, for instance, the analysis of the responses to the Learning Style Survey (Cohen et al., 2002) showed that the learner's preferred learning styles (e.g., she turned out to be an introverted, visual or concrete-sequential learner) had a role to play in her experience of boredom in the context of the virtual world SL.

Kruk (2021b)

In his mixed-methods study involving six female students of English philology, Kruk (2021b) examined the causes of and changes in the experience of boredom and language anxiety (alongside willingness to communicate and motivation) in the virtual world SL both during single sessions and from one session to another over one semester. Additionally, the researcher's attention was directed to possible relationships among the investigated emotions, the students' desire to communicate and their motivation. The data were gathered through a session log (it contained four grids in which the participants were asked to self-rate their level of language anxiety, boredom, willingness to communicate and motivation, as well as a space provided for a description of a session), a semi-structured interview and the Learning Style Survey (Cohen et al., 2002). The results of the study revealed the dynamic nature of the investigated variables in the case of each participant, that is, changes in their levels were observed both during an individual visit to SL and from visit to visit. However, the general trends recorded for the variables in question often did not correspond with those observed in individual participants and in the case of individual sessions. The findings also showed that the levels of language anxiety and boredom (as well as willingness to communicate and motivation) varied from session to session, both in the case of the phenomena under investigation and in individual participants. It was also

42 *Research on positive and negative emotions*

revealed that the variables formed unique constellations, both during single sessions and over time. Although, in the case of the former, a higher/lower level of WTC and motivation translated into a lower/higher level of experiencing boredom and language anxiety, these relationships were not the norm. When it comes to the latter, in addition to certain relationships (e.g., similar overall high levels of WTC and motivation and an accompanying low level of the experience of boredom), some deviations from the general trend were also observed. The qualitative analysis of the collected data uncovered a number of factors influencing the levels of language anxiety and boredom (as well as WTC and motivation), which were grouped into positive and negative. Some of the identified factors (e.g., SL users) were common to the negative emotions under investigation and the participants, while some others were characteristic of a given emotion (e.g., boredom: conversation topics; language anxiety: confidence, making mistakes) and a particular student participating in the study. The results also showed that the presence and/or fluctuations in the level of a given emotion depended on the participants' preferred learning style.

Kruk (2021c)

The investigation of the changing nature of language anxiety in the context of the virtual world SL and the factors influencing its variability were the aims of the study carried out by Kruk (2021c). The quantitative analysis of the data collected through a language anxiety grid (i.e., a tool in which the student was requested to self-rate her level of language anxiety at the beginning, middle and end of each session in SL on a seven-point scale) for each of the 14 sessions completed by the participant (i.e., a second-year student of English philology) revealed a changing nature of the investigated negative emotion. More specifically, the intensity of language anxiety varied from session to session and during individual visits. It should also be added that its levels largely corresponded to the overall tendency of the participant to experience anxiety when performing language tasks in SL. Qualitative analysis of the data obtained by means of the descriptions of sessions and a semi-structured interview allowed identification of a number of factors responsible for temporal variation in foreign language anxiety. Among others, the participant experienced increased anxiety when she communicated with people she did not know, participated in group chats, or could not find willing and/or talkative SL residents. By contrast, the learner experienced less anxiety when she communicated with previously met SL users, talked to SL users who were not fluent in English, or when she noticed that her interlocutors did not pay attention to the quality of the TL used.

Lee and Lee (2021)

In their interdisciplinary research project, Lee and Lee (2021) set out to scrutinize the relationship among the Informal Digital Learning of English

Research on positive and negative emotions 43

(IDLE), the L2 Motivational Self System (comprising the ideal L2 self and the ought-to L2 self; cf. Csizér, 2020; Dörnyei, 2009) and foreign language enjoyment (FLE). The participants were 661 Korean EFL middle and high school learners as well as university students who completed an online questionnaire tapping into the constructs under investigation. The quantitative analysis of the collected data revealed a greater propensity to enjoy learning English in the case of individuals who (1) exhibited a stronger ideal L2 self-image, (2) practiced IDLE activities, and (3) comprised middle school learners and learned English to meet the expectations of their significant others (e.g., teachers, peers and parents). According to the researchers, the results indicate that language learners' engagement in extramural digital activities and their motivational mindset may have affected their emotions in learning the English language. Based on the findings, Lee and Lee (2021) suggested that language teachers may try to heighten language learning enjoyment by encouraging students to learn an L2 in out-of-class digital settings as well as fostering their ideal L2 self-images.

Derakhshan, Kruk, Mehdizadeh and Pawlak (2021)

The study conducted by Derakhshan and colleagues (2021) set out to explore causes of and solutions to the experience of boredom, as well as the time of class regarded more and/or less boring in online classes held during the Covid-19 health crisis. The participants were 208 English major students in Iran. The required data were gathered via a written, open-ended online questionnaire and semi-structured interviews. Qualitative analysis showed that the experience of the aversive emotion in question in online classes was mostly induced by factors that were (1) teacher-related, (2) IT/computer-related, (3) task-related, and (4) student-related. As for the first set of factors, it included teachers' with-it-ness, that is, the state of being on top of things (McEwan, 2002), their instructional practices and personality (e.g., teachers' long, monotonous monologues, lack of student involvement, and carelessly selected, repetitive language tasks). The second set of factors comprised the causes that came from the specificity of the online learning and encompassed the logistics of online learning, the nature of online classes and IT/computer illiteracy (e.g., poor internet connection, lack of face-to-face interaction and teacher/student illiteracy). The third factor encompassed boring topics, dull materials, task overload, lack of comprehensible input, task difficulty and lack of task variety. Finally, the student-related factors were linked to students' physical fatigue, peers' irrelevant talk, and unmotivated individuals. The results also revealed a number of suggested solutions to boredom in online classes that revolved around making the class livelier (e.g., making breaks and offering interesting/authentic materials), improving IT infrastructure and individuals' IT know-how (e.g., solving logistic issues and improving individuals' technology literacy), involving students in discussions and encouraging participation, improving interpersonal relationships and lifestyle changes (e.g., exercising and getting fresh air). The results of the study also demonstrated that although the

44 *Research on positive and negative emotions*

experience of the negative emotion of boredom may be felt throughout online English classes, even at the very beginning, it has a tendency to reach its climax toward the end.

Sampson and Yoshida (2021)

Sampson and Yoshida (2021) set out to identify the feelings experienced by a group of EFL students during online text chat by means of the messaging application LINE. The participants included a group of undergraduates studying English as a foreign language at a university in Japan and a cohort of Japanese foreign language undergraduates from a university in Australia. The data were accumulated over the seven-week exchange by means of reflective session reports. These reports requested the participants to describe their feelings about communication in chat exchanges, their perceptions of communication skills, linguistic and cultural features, as well as issues concerning positive or negative parts in the chats. The students were requested to take part in chat sessions and interact for 30 minutes in their first language and 30 minutes in their second language. The analysis of the data revealed 11 distinct emotions. More specifically, there were seven positively (i.e., enjoyment, interest, a sense of achievement or progress, feelings of being motivated, gratitude, surprise and excitement) and four negatively (i.e., anxiety, a sense of difficulty/frustration, boredom/fatigue and disappointment) valenced feelings experienced by the language learners during L2 online chat. In both groups of students, the number of mentions regarding positive emotions exceeded that concerning the negative ones. They were linked with a variety of object-foci including, for instance, interests, L2 identity, themes relating to culture, dissimilarities in life experiences, linguistic features of the L2, the chat process and interlocutors.

Yazdanmehr, Elahi Shirvan and Saghafi (2021)

Yazdanmehr et al. (2021) employed a process-tracing approach to investigate the causal mechanisms of the negative emotion of boredom reported by one adult language learner in an online course in German as an L3 during the Covid-19 pandemic. The study spanned the period of one semester and encompassed 13 90-minute sessions. The data were collected by means of the following research instruments: a semi-structured interview, a journal and a boredometer. During the semi-structured interview, which was held after each session, the student was requested to describe her experience of learning German and her perceptions of the German classes she attended. As for the journal, the learner was asked to describe her feelings associated with boredom experienced in each session. Finally, the boredometer, that is, a thermometer-shaped drawing with a scale ranging from 0 (lowest level) to 10 (highest level), was used by the participant to indicate her level of the negative emotion in question every 30 minutes during each German class. The analysis of the

Research on positive and negative emotions 45

gathered data revealed that the aversive emotion under study displayed variation in duration and intensity from the initial phase of the language course to the final one. Furthermore, the study yielded theoretical and nontheoretical explanations of boredom. The former, related to understimulation, control/ value and attention deficit theories, could be used to account for boredom occurring from the start to the end of the course, while the latter, related to the user-unfriendly requirements of online education, which instigated physical and cognitive boredom, happened mostly in the initial phase of the course, were prevalent in the middle phase but were found to be less prominent towards the end.

Fraschini and Tao (2021)

Fraschini and Tao (2021) conducted an exploratory study aimed at investigating language learners' emotions in synchronous online teaching via Zoom. In addition, the study aimed at examining the correlations between learner emotions and academic achievement as well as crucial learner and teacher variables. A group of 117 students in an Australian university attending a Korean language course filled out an online Achievement Emotions Questionnaire consisting of 33 items related to the participants' background information, teacher friendliness and strictness, perceived classroom participation, as well as the feelings of enjoyment, pride and anxiety. The survey was administered four times throughout a semester. Among other things, the results of the study demonstrated that the patterns of the relationship between learner emotions and learning outcomes in online contexts were comparable to those in offline contexts. More specifically, positive outcomes tended to be related to enjoyment and pride, whereas negative outcomes displayed a tendency to be linked with anxiety. Furthermore, the findings showed that the feelings of enjoyment and anxiety may well co-occur in L2 learning, but also that learner emotions may be associated with achievement in learning the TL. The results also uncovered differences in experiencing emotions during online language learning by students with different characteristics. More specifically, the findings demonstrated that prior experience of learning an L2 can lessen the perceived challenges of learning another language, although such experience seems to have little influence on enjoyment and pride. It was also found that teacher friendliness is one of the strongest predictors of enjoyment in learning an L2.

Resnik and Dewaele (2021)

Resnik and Dewaele (2021) set out to explore the impact of the abrupt introduction of emergency remote teaching (ERT) after the spread of the Covid-19 pandemic on the positive and negative emotions experienced by 510 tertiary-level EFL students. The study was guided by three research questions related to the extent to which foreign language enjoyment and foreign

46 *Research on positive and negative emotions*

language anxiety varied in traditional (i.e., taught in person) and online classes, the relationship between the participants' enjoyment and anxiety in each setting and across both settings, as well as the links between trait emotional intelligence (TEI), learner autonomy and the students' emotions in both contexts. The data were collected with the help of a web survey containing sets of questions regarding the respondents' demographics, their previous experience with online learning, items related to the feelings of enjoyment and anxiety in learning an L2 in traditional and online classes, as well as learner autonomy. The questionnaire was also accompanied by two optional open-ended questions that queried the students about other emotions they felt in the settings in question and perceived differences between the two contexts. Among other things, the results showed that the participants regarded both traditional and online classes as more enjoyable and less anxiety inducing; however, their feelings of enjoyment were significantly lower in online contexts than in conventional classes. The results also showed that, in general, the levels of enjoyment and anxiety in learning a foreign language were positively correlated between both settings. It was also found that the respondents who were characterized by high levels of TEI experienced more enjoyment and less anxiety in learning the target language in both contexts. TEI and learner autonomy were positively linked and they were positively and negatively connected to enjoyment and anxiety in both settings. Last but not least, the findings revealed that more autonomous learners enjoyed learning the target language more than their less autonomous counterparts in both contexts. Resnik and Dewaele concluded that although the use of technology after the outbreak of the Covid-19 pandemic allowed the continuation of language education, reliance on online classes tended to "dull students' emotions" since "disembodied classes have less emotional resonance" (p. 21).

Conclusion

The present chapter has offered an overview of the available research into positive and negative emotions in L2 learning and teaching in traditional and CALL contexts. The first section included a synthesis of studies referring to the research projects on the positive emotions of curiosity and enjoyment and the negative emotions of anxiety and boredom in learning and teaching an L2 in traditional settings. The discussed studies approached the emotions in question from different angles, which is reflected, for instance, in different numbers of participants, the diversity of research instruments employed and the procedures of data analysis. In addition, some of these studies focused on different target languages and the relationships of different emotions and/or variables over different time frames as well as changes in the levels of the four emotions and factors responsible for such variations. When it comes to the second section, it provided an overview of empirical investigations focused on the positive and negative emotions involved in L2 learning and teaching in CALL contexts. In view of the fact that language anxiety has been extensively investigated in the field of CALL, a description of some of the most recent research projects regarding the said negative emotion has been offered, along with a description of the available studies that sought to examine the emerging negative emotion of boredom and some other positive emotions such as, for example, enjoyment, curiosity and pride. The synthesis included in the second section has also demonstrated the paucity of research into emotion in L2 learning and teaching in the context of CALL, as well as the methodological limitations of many such investigations. For this reason, there is clearly an urgent need to undertake more studies that would tap into the role of positive and negative emotions in online settings, also paying attention to their dynamics and the factors responsible for their fluctuations. The following chapter is dedicated in its entirety to describing the methodology of a research project that was carried out with the purpose of shedding light on these issues.

3 Methodology of the research project

Introduction

Chapter 1 and Chapter 2 have offered an overview of selected theoretical issues as well as a synthesis of research projects regarding the positive and negative emotions impacting second language (L2) learning and teaching in traditional and computer-assisted language learning (CALL) contexts, thus offering a backdrop to the study reported in the remainder of the present volume. More specifically, the first chapter concentrated on the role of emotions in conventional settings and CALL, as well as the presentation of the definitions of the emotions investigated in the present study, their types, dimensions and sources. The second chapter, in turn, was devoted to an overview of research projects concerning positive and negative emotions, both those that have been undertaken in the traditional contexts of L2 learning and teaching and those that have targeted these emotions in CALL settings. As signaled in the conclusion to the previous chapter, even a cursory look at the empirical investigations in the field of CALL, particularly with regard to emotions other than foreign language anxiety, conducted thus far shows that the available empirical evidence is scarce and further research needs to be carried out in order to gain more insights into the occurrence of both positive and negative emotions in CALL contexts. Equally important is shedding more light on the degree to which the experience of these emotions by L2 learners is stable or, rather, tends to change at different timescales, as well as the sources of these variations, in the hope of offering suggestions as to how it can be nurtured or, conversely, combated in CALL settings. This is the rationale for the study conducted for the purpose of this book. The present chapter presents the design, methodology and implementation of such an investigation that was intended to provide insights into the role of the positive emotions of curiosity and enjoyment and the negative emotions of anxiety and boredom in L2 learning in online settings. The chapter presents the aims of the study and the research questions, the description of the participants, the procedures and language activities the learners performed in the virtual world Second Life (SL), a detailed description of the research instruments by means of which the data were gathered, and the ways in which these data were analyzed.

DOI: 10.4324/9781003240068-4

Methodology of the research project 49

Aims and research questions

The aim of this research project was to explore the positive emotions of curiosity and enjoyment and the negative emotions of boredom and anxiety experienced by 16 English majors in the virtual world Second Life. More specifically, the study was intended to shed light on the overall intensity of these emotions, changes in this intensity and the main factors influencing the occurrence of these emotions, as well as their relationships. The investigation of such issues was conducted with respect to three distinct student profiles determined on the basis of their overall propensity to experience the four emotions under investigation. Importantly, the distinctiveness of this study pertains to the fact that it sought to examine issues specified above among students who used SL over several weeks in the summer semester of 2020 in informal contexts, the period when the coronavirus pandemic rendered face-to-face L2 education impossible in many settings. More specifically, the following research questions were formulated:

1 What levels of the positive (i.e., curiosity and enjoyment) and negative (i.e., boredom and anxiety) emotions do students report and what distinct student profiles can be identified on this basis? (RQ1)
2 What are the overall levels of the positive and negative emotions experienced by the participants in SL? (RQ2)
3 How do the levels of positive and negative emotions change from one visit to SL to the next? (RQ3)
4 What is the relationship between and/or among the positive and negative emotions in question and is it subject to temporal variation? (RQ4)
5 What factors cause the positive and negative emotions and what influences are responsible for changes in the experience of these emotions? (RQ5)

Participants

The participants were 16 English majors, 13 females and 3 males, enrolled in the second year of a three-year Bachelor of Arts program at a Polish university located in a medium-sized town in Poland. The students were, on average, 20.69 ($SD = .79$) years old. They were required to attend an intensive course in English, divided into classes focusing on developing English language skills and subsystems (e.g., listening, reading, writing, speaking, grammar), content classes (e.g., linguistics, applied linguistics, literature, history, language teaching methodology) as well as electives (e.g., proseminars, specialized courses), most of which were taught in English. The mean experience in learning the target language (TL) was 13.19 years, with the standard deviation value of 2.04, which indicates some individual variation in this respect. As far as participants' TL proficiency is concerned, the students could be roughly described as representing the B2 level, as defined in the *Common*

50 *Methodology of the research project*

European Framework (Council of Europe, 2001), but there was some individual variation in this case as well. In terms of the grading systems used in institutions of higher education in Poland, the mean grade on the final examination in English, administered at the end of the first year, was 3.88 ($SD = .67$) on a scale from 2 (lowest) to 5 (highest). The participants' self-evaluation of their TL ability was comparable (3.84; $SD = .35$) on the same scale. Particularly relevant to this study was the learners' self-assessment of their face-to-face and computer-mediated communication (CMC) skills, which were 3.56 ($SD = .51$) and 3.75 ($SD = .58$), respectively, on the scale already referenced above. In addition, 15 out of 16 students reported taking part in CMC, mostly for pleasure and/or social reasons. Even though the majority of the participants reported using CMC, most of them (nine students) had not heard of a virtual world before the study was conducted, only five had visited a virtual world, and no one had actually used a virtual world for improving their English proficiency (e.g., in order to interact with learners of English or English native speakers). More specific information about the participants is presented in Table 3.1.

Based on the participants' responses to a set of scales, that is, the Language Learning Curiosity Scale (LLCS), the Language Learning Enjoyment Scale (LLES), the Boredom in Practical English Language Classes – Revised (BPELC-R) scale and the Foreign Language Classroom Anxiety (FLCA) scale (for details see p. 64 in Chapter 4) and their interpretation (Wattana, 2013; for details see p. 57), the participants were divided into three groups for the purpose of the present study: (1) students who displayed very high or high levels of two positive emotions vs. neutral or low levels of two negative emotions, (2) participants who manifested a very high or high level of one positive emotion vs. neutral or low levels of negative and positive emotions, and (3) individuals who represented a mixture of high/neutral/low levels of positive and/or negative emotions. More specific information about the participants included in the three groups can be found in Table 3.1. More detailed information about each group follows:

- Group 1: seven students (five females and two males); average age 20.29 ($SD = .49$); experience in learning English 13.71 years ($SD = 2.14$); average grade on the end-of-the-year examination in English and their self-assessment of English proficiency were 3.79 ($SD = .81$) and 4.00 ($SD = .29$), respectively; all students reported taking part in CMC and used it mostly for pleasure and social reasons; their average self-rating of face-to-face and CMC skills were 3.86 ($SD = .38$) and 4.00 ($SD = .58$), respectively; four learners (Aurora, Debra, Emma and Addison) had heard of a virtual world and three individuals (Aurora, Debra and Addison) had visited such an environment, but none had used it for learning English before the study; four students (Debra, Emma, Jack and David) demonstrated high levels of language learning curiosity and enjoyment and neutral levels of boredom and foreign language anxiety, two learners (Abigail and Addison) exhibited high levels of language learning curiosity and enjoyment, a neutral level of

Table 3.1 Participants of the study

Participant (pseudonyms)	Sex: F = female M = male	Age	The length of English study	Grade received on the end-of-the-year examination in English	Self-assessment of English proficiency	Taking part in CMC	The use of CMC P = for pleasure S = social reasons I = intentionally improve English	Self-rating of face-to-face communication skills: from 2 (lowest) to 5 (highest)	Self-rating of CMC skills: from 2 (lowest) to 5 (highest)	Ever heard of a virtual world (e.g., Second Life)	Ever visited a virtual world (e.g., Second Life)	Ever used a virtual world (e.g., Second Life) for learning English
							M (SD)					
Aurora	F	20	14	4.5	4	Yes	pleasure	4	4	Yes	Yes	No
Debra	F	21	17	5	4.5	Yes	social, intentionally	4	4	Yes	Yes	No
Emma	F	20	13	3	4	Yes	pleasure	4	4	Yes	No	No
Jack	M	20	14	4	4	Yes	social	4	5	No	No	No
David	M	20	13	3	4	Yes	social	4	4	No	No	No
Abigail	F	21	10	3	3.5	Yes	pleasure, social	3	3	No	No	No
Addison	F	20	15	4	4	Yes	social	4	4	Yes	Yes	No
Group 1	F: 5, M: 2	20.29 (.49)	13.71 (2.14)	3.79 (.81)	4.00 (.29)	Yes: 7 No: 0	P: 3, S: 5, I: 1	3.86 (.38)	4.00 (.58)	Yes: 4 No: 3	Yes: 3 No: 4	Yes: 0 No: 7
Ava	F	20	11	3.5	4	Yes	pleasure	4	4	No	No	No
Jakob	M	21	12	4.5	4	Yes	social	4	4	No	No	No
Isabella	F	20	12	4	4	Yes	social	3	4	Yes	No	No
Olivia	F	21	14	4	3.5	Yes	social	3	3	No	No	No
Hazel	F	21	14	3.5	3.5	Yes	pleasure, social	3	3	No	No	No
Amelia	F	20	13	3	3	No		3	3	Yes	No	No
Group 2	F: 5, M: 1	20.50 (.55)	12.67 (1.21)	3.75 (.52)	3.67 (.41)	Yes: 5 No: 1	P: 2, S: 4, I: 0	3.33 (.52)	3.50 (.55)	Yes: 2 No: 4	Yes: 0 No: 6	Yes: 0 No: 6

Participant (pseudonyms)	Sex: F = female M = male	Age	The length of English study	Grade received on the end-of-the-year examination in English	Self-assessment of English proficiency	Taking part in CMC	The use of CMC P = for pleasure S = social reasons I = intentionally improve English	Self-rating of face-to-face communication skills: from 2 (lowest) to 5 (highest)	Self-rating of CMC skills: from 2 (lowest) to 5 (highest)	Ever heard of a virtual world (e.g., Second Life)	Ever visited a virtual world (e.g., Second Life)	Ever used a virtual world (e.g., Second Life) for learning English
Gianna	F	22	15	5	4	Yes	pleasure	4	4	No	No	No
Sophia	F	22	15	4	4	Yes	pleasure	3	4	No	No	No
Grace	F	22	9	4	3.5	Yes	pleasure	3	3	Yes	Yes	No
Group 3	F: 3	22.00 (.00)	13.00 (3.46)	4.33 (.58)	3.83 (.29)	Yes: 3 No: 0	P: 3, S: 0, I: 0	3.33 (.58)	3.67 (.58)	Yes: 1 No: 2	Yes: 1 No: 2	Yes: 0 No: 3
Total	F: 13, M: 3	20.69 (.79)	13.19 (2.04)	3.88 (.67)	3.84 (.35)	Yes: 15 No: 1	P: 8, S: 9, I: 1	3.56 (.51)	3.75 (.58)	Yes: 7 No: 9	Yes: 5 No: 12	Yes: 0 No: 16

Methodology of the research project   53

foreign language anxiety and low intensity of boredom in the classroom, whereas one individual (Aurora) showed very high levels of curiosity and enjoyment and neutral levels of boredom and language anxiety.

- Group 2: six students (five females and one male); average age 20.50 (*SD* = .55); experience in learning English 12.67 years (*SD* = 1.21); average grade on the end-of-the-year examination in English and their self-assessment of English proficiency were 3.75 (*SD* = .52) and 3.67 (*SD* = .41), respectively; five students (Ava, Jakob, Isabella, Olivia and Hazel) took part in CMC and used it for social reasons (Jakob, Isabella and Olivia), pleasure (Ava) and both social reasons and pleasure (Hazel); their average self-rating of face-to-face and CMC skills were 3.33 (*SD* = .52) and 3.50 (*SD* = .55), respectively; two individuals (Isabella and Amelia) had heard of a virtual world but had not visited it; no one had used a virtual world for learning English before the study; one learner (Ava) displayed a very high level of curiosity but neutral levels of language learning enjoyment, boredom and language anxiety, four students (Jacob, Isabella, Olivia and Hazel) showed a high level of curiosity and a low level of language learning enjoyment, boredom and anxiety, whereas one participant (Amelia) demonstrated a high level of enjoyment and neutral levels of language learning curiosity, boredom and anxiety.
- Group 3: three female students; average age 22.00 (*SD* = .00); experience in learning English 13.00 years (*SD* = 3.46); average grade on the end-of-the-year examination in English and their self-assessment of English proficiency were 4.33 (*SD* = .58) and 3.83 (*SD* = .29), respectively; all students took part in CMC and used it for pleasure; their average self-ratings of face-to-face and CMC skills were 3.33 (*SD* = .58) and 3.67 (*SD* = .58), respectively; one individual (Grace) had heard of a virtual world and had visited it but no one used it for learning English before the study; one student (Gianna) exhibited high levels of language learning curiosity and anxiety but neutral levels of enjoyment and boredom in the language classroom, one student (Sophia) demonstrated high levels of language learning curiosity, enjoyment and anxiety but a low level of boredom, and one individual (Grace) manifested high levels of language learning curiosity and boredom but neutral levels of language learning enjoyment and anxiety.

Data collection instruments

The requisite data were gathered by means of several instruments, some of which were modifications of research tools utilized in previous empirical investigations carried out by the present authors. These involved a background questionnaire, questionnaires intended to tap into the positive and negative emotions under investigation and an in-world session log. It should be made clear at this juncture that English was used in all the research tools as it was assumed that as the participants of the present study were English majors, they had a sufficient level of TL proficiency to provide the necessary

54 *Methodology of the research project*

responses. The background questionnaire, the questionnaires concerning positive and negative feelings and the in-world session log took the form of Microsoft Word documents, which were filled out electronically and subsequently sent to one of the researchers by email. These tools are described in detail below.

Background questionnaire

The main purpose of the background questionnaire (see Appendix A) was to obtain general information regarding the students who participated in the study. The questionnaire included questions related to the participants' sex, age, the length of English instruction, grades received on the comprehensive end-of-the-year examination in English and self-assessment of English proficiency, the students' use of CMC on a daily basis, their self-evaluation of their face-to-face and CMC skills as well as their use of virtual worlds for language learning, in particular the learning of English.

Questionnaires on positive and negative emotions

Four scales (see Appendix B) measuring positive and negative emotions involved in learning a foreign language in the traditional settings were used in the present study. What follows is a description of each tool together with relevant Cronbach's alpha values calculated for the sample involved in this study and interpreted in accordance with Dörnyei (2007):

- the Language Learning Curiosity Scale (LLCS) created by Mahmoodzadeh and Khajavy (2019); the scale includes 11 five-point Likert-scale statements (1 – disagree strongly and 5 – agree strongly) divided into two subscales: (1) language curiosity as a feeling of interest (four items; e.g., "I wonder how well I can speak English in contexts outside the classroom," "I always like to know how to use the new words I learn in conversational situations outside the classroom") and (2) language curiosity as a feeling of deprivation (seven items; e.g., "I always like to learn not only the language rules but also the exceptions," "When I have a language question in mind, I cannot rest without knowing the answer"); the internal consistency of the questionnaire, determined by Cronbach's α, was 0.64, a value that can be viewed as acceptable (cf. Dörnyei, 2007).
- the Language Learning Enjoyment Scale (LLES), taken from Mahmoodzadeh and Khajavy (2019), which they adapted from Dewaele and MacIntyre (2014) and Peixoto et al. (2015); the scale includes eight five-point Likert-scale statements (1 – disagree strongly and 5 – agree strongly) regarding various facets of language learning enjoyment, such as fun, interest, relief, hope and pride (e.g., "I feel excited about being in my language class listening to the teacher," "In my language class, I feel proud of my accomplishments"); the reliability for the overall scale was acceptable (cf. Dörnyei, 2007), with a Cronbach's α value of 0.75.

Methodology of the research project 55

- the Boredom in Practical English Language Classes – Revised (BPELC-R) scale, developed and validated by Pawlak et al. (2020b); the scale includes 23 five-point Likert-scale statements (1 – disagree strongly and 5 – agree strongly), such as: "It takes more stimulation to get me going in English classes than most students from my group," "If I am not doing something interesting/exciting during English classes, I feel tired and bored," "Having to listen to my English language teachers present material bores me tremendously"; Cronbach's α for this measure was 0.82, a value that can be viewed as satisfactory (cf. Dörnyei, 2007).
- the Foreign Language Classroom Anxiety (FLCA) scale used by Dewaele and MacIntyre (2014) on the basis of FLCAS (Horwitz et al., 1986); the scale includes eight five-point Likert-scale statements (1 – disagree strongly and 5 – agree strongly), such as: "I always feel that the other students speak the foreign language better than I do," "I can feel my heart pounding when I'm going to be called on in a language class"; Cronbach's α for this scale was 0.62, a value that can be viewed as satisfactory for such a short scale (Dörnyei, 2007).

In-world session log

The in-world session log (see Appendix C) consisted of two parts. Part One required the students to write in English a description of each session in SL in which they took part. They were asked to write about their enjoyment concerning learning English during visits and if they felt curious about learning English in SL. The students were also asked to write about the experience of boredom and language anxiety in each visit. The participants were asked to consider a set of questions related to the issues under investigation. These were the following:

What did you enjoy the most?
What were you curious about?
Who/What made you bored?
When did you feel bored?
Who/What made you anxious?
When did you feel particularly anxious?

Part Two included the emotional grid in which the learners were requested to self-rate their language learning curiosity, enjoyment, boredom and anxiety on a scale ranging from 1 (minimum) to 5 (maximum). The in-world session log was completed by the participants after each session in SL. As mentioned above, the in-world log was modeled on similar instruments developed by the present authors and used in empirical investigations (e.g., Kruk, 2016a, 2021b; Mystkowska-Wiertelak & Pawlak, 2017; Pawlak, 2012; Pawlak et al., 2020a).

Research procedures and activities in SL

As can be seen in Figure 3.1, prior to data collection all the participants gave their consent to take part in the study on a voluntarily basis. In addition, the learners were informed that they could withdraw from the study at any time. Subsequently, the students were asked to fill out a background questionnaire as well as instruments tapping into the positive and negative emotions under investigation. The instruments were prepared in a Word document, sent to the participants by email, completed electronically and sent back to one of the researchers through email. This was followed by an online orientation session. During this session the participants were provided with necessary information regarding the use of the virtual world SL. They were, among other things, shown how to create an account, create a personal avatar and move around the nooks and corners of the virtual world. More specifically, they were instructed how to walk, run, jump, teleport to different places, etc. It was also explained to them how to communicate with SL users by means of text chat (e.g., synchronous public text or group text chat) and voice channels (i.e., public, group, or private ones) as well as how to interact with objects within SL. As far language activities are concerned, the participants were offered some language tasks to be performed in SL; however, due to the fact that they agreed to use SL in their own time, the participants were also encouraged to invent their own L2 learning activities and simply use the opportunity to practice their English language skills the way they deemed optimal. As regards the L2 tasks devised by the researchers, they were the following:

- Casual chats with SL users: while exploring SL try to find SL users (including your classmates) who are willing to interact in English and discuss topics of your own choice (e.g., your interests, current news, places in SL).
- Comparing the real world with the virtual world SL: discuss with SL users (including your classmates) the similarities and differences between the real world and the virtual world SL.
- The quality of life in SL: Pretend to be a journalist working for a local newspaper. Your assignment is to write an article on the quality of life in SL. Talk to SL residents (including your classmates) about

Figure 3.1 Research procedures and activities in SL

Methodology of the research project 57

their opinions on SL, their positive and/or negative experience of living in SL, etc.

- Talking about differences of living in big cities before and now – 1920s–1940s New York in Time Portal: use the time portal and discuss differences concerning life in big cities before and now with SL users (including your classmates).

After each visit to SL the students were requested to electronically complete the in-world session log (also designed as a Word document; see p. 55 for information about its design) and send it to the same researcher by email.

Data analysis

Quantitative analysis

The quantitative data, which originated from the background questionnaire, the questionnaires relating to positive and negative emotions in the traditional context and the in-world emotional grid (i.e., the second part of the in-world session log), underwent quantitative analysis. This took the form of running basic descriptive statistics that involved calculating the mean and standard deviation values for all students, groups and individual learners. The levels of language learning curiosity, enjoyment, boredom and anxiety were interpreted according to the range of mean scores included in Table 3.2 (cf. Wattana, 2013).

Taking into consideration the exploratory character of the study, the relatively small number of participants, and the research questions posed, it was decided not to employ inferential statistics. The main reason was the fact that the study did not aim to prove the existence of any statistically significant differences in the reported intensity of positive and negative emotions but, rather, shed light on their overall levels and their interactions in L2 learning in an online setting. In addition, the research project involved a small sample of participants ($N = 16$) who, in general, performed different language activities (i.e., they decided on activities to be performed in each session) and who availed themselves of various numbers of visits of different length as well as character.

Table 3.2 The interpretation of mean scores for the levels of language learning curiosity, enjoyment, boredom and anxiety

Range of mean scores	*Interpretation*
4.50–5.00	**Very high** level of curiosity, enjoyment, boredom, anxiety
3.50–4.49	**High** level of curiosity, enjoyment, boredom, anxiety
2.50–3.49	**Neutral** level of curiosity, enjoyment, boredom, anxiety
1.50–2.49	**Low** level of curiosity, enjoyment, boredom, anxiety
1.00–1.49	**Very low** level of curiosity, enjoyment, boredom, anxiety

58 *Methodology of the research project*

Qualitative analysis

The qualitative analysis was focused on the students' descriptions of their sessions in SL, that is, their responses to the first part of the in-world session log, and it followed the procedure used in earlier studies conducted by Kruk (e.g., Kruk, 2019, 2021b). The analysis commenced with a thorough reading of the narratives in order to achieve an overall sense of the data. Altogether, the students generated a total of 14,471 words (for details see Table 3.3, which shows the number of words for each student). Next, both researchers repeatedly read the narratives produced by each participant (i.e., the data were read for each participant separately) in order to identify excerpts that could inform the issues included in the relevant research questions (i.e., relationships between the positive and negative emotions under investigation). In the process, notes and annotations were made and pertinent codes were applied. The preliminary codes were then combined and revised. The data were analyzed by the present researchers separately. Any disagreements regarding interpretation and/or categorization were discussed and resolved. The inter-coder agreement reached 92%, which is considered to be satisfactory (Miles & Huberman, 1994). What should be emphasized at this point is that the data excerpts reported in the findings give a voice to participants and, in this way, they add an emic dimension (Dewaele, 2009) to the quantitative results and the students' language learning endeavors in SL.

Table 3.3 Student narratives

Student	Number of sessions	Words produced
Aurora	5	1,808
Debra	4	704
Emma	8	1,464
Jack	4	415
David	4	490
Abigail	5	729
Addison	3	812
Ava	7	1,237
Jacob	5	1,008
Isabella	5	855
Olivia	5	764
Hazel	3	1,341
Amelia	3	432
Gianna	5	794
Sophia	5	690
Grace	6	928
Total	**77**	**14,471**

Methodology of the research project 59

Conclusion

The present chapter has offered a description of the aims of the study, its participants, design, data collection instruments and the procedures by means of which the collected data were analyzed. Since the study included a small sample that comprised only 16 students and involved a limited number of sessions in SL, it could be argued that a larger sample and a larger number of sessions may have supplied more data. Nevertheless, it was the belief of the present authors that the implementation of diverse research instruments and scrupulous ways of data analysis were an effective way of obtaining invaluable and in-depth insights into understanding the positive and negative emotions experienced by the participants in their language endeavors in the virtual world SL. This approach is consistent with micro-perspective as it enabled the investigation of the emotions under study in a specific, computer-generated environment with the aid of information obtained from a number of sources, thus uncovering the complex relationships between emotions and factors influencing them, which by their very nature are difficult to grasp in any context. The following chapter will present the findings of this research endeavor as well as their interpretation in the light of the research questions posed.

4 Research findings

Introduction

The aim of the present chapter is to report the results of the study and to offer a discussion of its findings. The focus will be on the outcomes of the in-depth analysis of the quantitative and qualitative data. At the outset, overall results of the LLCS, LLES, BPELC-R and FLCA scales regarding the traditional context for the entire group will be examined and three distinct student profiles will be identified on this basis. Subsequently, the focus will be shifted to the general levels of the four emotions under investigation indicated on a grid by the participants included in the in-world session log. More specifically, the findings will be presented in the following order: (1) overall levels of the four emotions for the entire sample in the traditional context, (2) general levels of the four emotions for individual participants in the traditional settings, (3) self-reported levels of the emotions in question for the entire sample in Second Life (SL), (4) self-reported levels of the four emotions within Group 1, Group 2 and Group 3 in SL, and (5) differences in self-reported levels of the emotions under study from one visit to SL to the next for individual learners in the three groups. This will be followed by the presentation of the participants' emotional accounts of their visits to SL with regard to individual students within the three groups. The chapter will close with a discussion of the findings in terms of the research questions posed for the present research project along with the limitations of the study.

Quantitative findings

The present section will start with the presentation of overall levels of the positive and negative emotions reported by the entire sample and individual students when responding to the LLCS, LLES, BPELC-R and FLCA scales in traditional classroom settings. Subsequently, self-reported levels of the four emotions under study in SL reported by the entire sample as well as within Group 1, Group 2 and Group 3, and the differences in self-reported levels of the emotions in question from one session in the virtual world to another for individual participants in the three groups will be offered.

DOI: 10.4324/9781003240068-5

Research findings 61

General levels of positive and negative emotions for the entire group in traditional settings

The analysis of the aggregate responses to the LLCS, LLES, BPELC-R and FLCA scales for the entire sample (i.e., 16 participants) and interpreted according to Wattana (2013) (see p. 57 in Chapter 3) revealed that the levels of curiosity (M = 4.02) and enjoyment (M = 3.51) in learning English in the classroom can be considered high. By contrast, the participants experienced neutral levels of boredom (M = 2.75) and language anxiety (M = 3.08). It should also be noted that there was some individual variation in each emotion, as indicated by the value of standard deviation (LLCS: SD = .38, LLES: SD = .54, BPELC-R: SD = .40 and FLCA: SD = .44) (see Table 4.1).

Table 4.1 The mean and standard deviation values for the positive and negative emotions for the entire group in traditional context

Item	Language Learning Curiosity Scale (LLCS)	Language Learning Enjoyment Scale (LLES)	Boredom in Practical English Language Classes - Revised (BPELC-R)	Foreign Language Classroom Anxiety (FLCA)
			M (SD)	
1	3.63 (.81)	3.19 (.83)	3.19 (.54)	3.56 (1.31)
2	3.88 (.72)	3.63 (.81)	2.63 (.81)	3.25 (.86)
3	3.75 (1.06)	3.44 (.81)	2.81 (1.22)	3.38 (1.09)
4	4.31 (.79)	4.06 (.85)	3.13 (.89)	2.88 (1.15)
5	3.88 (.72)	3.31 (.87)	3.38 (.81)	3.06 (1.00)
6	4.13 (.81)	3.63 (.81)	2.50 (.82)	2.94 (1.00)
7	4.38 (.62)	3.38 (1.31)	3.50 (.82)	2.69 (1.08)
8	3.81 (1.11)	3.44 (.81)	2.94 (.85)	2.88 (1.02)
9	4.69 (.60)	-	2.50 (.73)	-
10	4.06 (.77)	-	2.63 (1.02)	-
11	3.75 (.77)	-	2.19 (.91)	-
12	-	-	3.44 (1.09)	-
13	-	-	2.50 (.63)	-
14	-	-	2.38 (1.02)	-
15	-	-	3.69 (1.14)	-
16	-	-	3.00 (.63)	-
17	-	-	2.63 (1.15)	-
18	-	-	2.25 (.68)	-
19	-	-	2.81 (1.11)	-
20	-	-	2.13 (.81)	-
21	-	-	2.31 (.60)	-
22	-	-	2.50 (.73)	-
23	-	-	2.25 (1.06)	-
Total M (SD)	4.02 (.38)	3.51 (.54)	2.75 (.40)	3.08 (.44)

62 *Research findings*

As can be seen from Table 4.1, the highest means (i.e., those exceeding the mean value for the entire scale, that is, 4.02) in LLCS were reported by the following items: 9 ("I wonder how it would feel to speak English as fluently as a native speaker does" – M = 4.69, SD = .60), 7 ("When my language teacher corrects my grammatical mistake, I am just curious to know why it is not correct" – M = 4.38, SD = .62), 4 ("I wonder how well I can speak English when meeting a native English speaker" – M = 4.31, SD = .79) and 6 ("I wonder how it would feel to speak and write English as well as my language teacher does" – M = 4.13, SD = .81). The means considerably below the overall mean of 4.02 calculated for LLCS applied to the following items: 1 ("I wonder how well I can speak English in contexts outside the classroom" – M = 3.63, SD = .81), 3 ("When I have a language question in mind, I cannot rest without knowing the answer" – M = 3.75, SD = 1.06) and 11 ("I always like to know how to use the new words I learn in conversational situations outside the classroom" – M = 3.75, SD = .77).

As regards LLES, the items with the highest scores, that is, those with the means substantially exceeding the overall mean of 3.51 for the scale in its entirety, were the following: 4 ("I am glad that it paid off to go to my language class" – M = 4.06, SD = .85), 2 ("I enjoy being in my language class" – M = 3.63, SD = .81) and 6 ("I am a worthy member of my language class" – M = 3.63, SD = .81). When it comes to items with the means much lower than the overall mean tabulated for the entire LLES (M = 3.51), they included item 1 ("I am motivated to go to my language class because it is exciting" – M = 3.19, SD = .83), item 5 ("I do not get bored whilst learning English because I enjoy myself in class" – M = 3.31, SD = .87) and item 7 ("I can laugh off embarrassing mistakes in my language class" – M = 3.38, SD = 1.31) (see Table 4.1).

As far as the BPELC-R is concerned, the results showed that items with the means considerably higher than the overall mean of 2.75 calculated for the entire scale and thus constituting a sign of high intensity of boredom were item 15 ("If I am not doing something interesting/exciting during English classes, I feel tired and bored" – M = 3.69, SD = 1.14), item 7 ("I get a kick out of most things I do in a language class" – M = 3.50, SD = .82), item 12 ("I would like to have more challenging things to do in my English classes" – M = 3.44, SD = 1.09), item 5 ("I often have to do repetitive or monotonous things in my language classes" – M = 3.38, SD = .81) and item 1 ("Time always seems to be passing slowly in my language classes" – M = 3.19, SD = .54). Conversely, the items with the means markedly lower than the overall mean of 2.75 calculated for the entire BPELC-R scale included the following items: 20 ("Having to listen to my English language teachers present material bores me tremendously" – M = 2.13, SD = .81), 11 ("It would be very hard for me to find an exciting task in language classes" – M = 2.19, SD = .91), 18 ("It is easy for me to concentrate on the activities in my English language classes" – M = 2.25, SD = .68), 23 ("In situations where I have to wait (e.g., for everyone to finish their task), I get very restless" – M = 2.25, SD = 1.06) and 21 ("I actively participate in English classes" – M = 2.31, SD = .60) (see Table 4.1).

Research findings 63

Finally, the results of the FLCA scale revealed the highest means, that is, the means considerably exceeding the overall mean of 3.08 calculated for the entire scale and thus indicating high and neutral levels of language anxiety, in the case of two items: item 1 ("Even if I am well prepared for my language class, I feel anxious about it" – M = 3.56, SD = 1.31) and item 3 ("I can feel my heart pounding when I'm going to be called on in a language class" – M = 3.38, SD = 1.09). The lowest means, that is, the means below the overall mean of 3.08 and thus reflective of a neutral level of language anxiety, concerned three items: item 7 ("I start to panic when I have to speak without preparation in my foreign language class" – M = 2.69, SD = 1.08), item 4 ("I don't worry about making mistakes in my foreign language class" – M = 2.88, SD = 1.15) and item 8 ("It embarrasses me to volunteer answers in my foreign language class" – M = 2.88, SD = 1.02) (see Table 4.1).

General levels of the positive and negative emotions for individual participants in traditional settings

As elucidated in the previous chapter, the participants' responses to the LLCS, LLES, BPELC-R and FLCA scales were also analyzed individually for each student. The means of their responses were calculated and then interpreted according to Wattana (2013) (see p. 57 in Chapter 3). As indicated in Table 4.2, the participants displayed varying levels of language learning curiosity, language learning enjoyment, the experience of boredom and language anxiety in the school settings. For example, Debra demonstrated high levels of curiosity (a mean of 3.82) and enjoyment (a mean of 3.50) in learning English, but displayed neutral levels of boredom (a mean of 2.61) and language anxiety (a mean of 2.50) in the traditional classroom. Ava demonstrated a very high level of language learning curiosity (a mean of 4.82) but neutral levels of language learning enjoyment, boredom and language anxiety (means of 3.00, 2.57 and 2.63, respectively). Sophia exhibited high levels of language learning curiosity (a mean of 3.73), enjoyment (a mean of 3.75) and anxiety (a mean of 3.75) but she did not experience a lot of boredom in learning the target language in the classroom (a mean of 2.13).

As mentioned on p. 50 , detailed inspection of the data included in Table 4.2 allowed dividing the participants into three groups: (1) participants who exhibited very high or high levels of two positive emotions vs. neutral or low levels of two negative emotions, (2) individuals who displayed a very high or high level of one positive emotion vs. neutral or low levels of negative and positive emotions, and (3) students who manifested a mixture of high/neutral/low levels of positive and/or negative emotions.

Self-reported levels of the positive and negative emotions for the entire sample in SL

Table 4.3 includes the overall levels of self-reported language learning curiosity (LLC), language learning enjoyment (LLE), the experience of language learning

64   Research findings

Table 4.2 The mean and standard deviation values for the positive and negative emotions in the case of individual students in traditional context

Student	LLCS	LLES	BPELC-R	FLCA
		M (SD)		
Debra	3.82 (.60)	3.50 (.53)	2.61 (.66)	2.50 (1.07)
Emma	4.09 (.70)	4.13 (.64)	2.61 (.78)	2.75 (.71)
Jack	3.91 (.94)	3.50 (.93)	2.96 (1.02)	2.63 (.74)
Ava	4.82 (.40)	3.00 (.93)	2.57 (.90)	2.63 (.74)
Gianna	4.09 (.83)	2.75 (.89)	3.30 (.97)	4.00 (1.85)
Sophia	3.73 (1.01)	3.75 (.71)	2.13 (.92)	3.75 (.71)
Jacob	3.82 (1.17)	3.25 (1.04)	2.65 (1.11)	3.38 (1.51)
Amelia	3.45 (.82)	3.63 (.52)	2.78 (.60)	3.38 (.52)
Isabella	4.18 (.75)	3.38 (.74)	2.61 (.99)	3.25 (.89)
Abigail	4.18 (.75)	3.88 (.64)	2.17 (1.03)	2.75 (.46)
David	3.73 (1.01)	3.88 (.99)	2.52 (1.24)	3.25 (1.28)
Olivia	4.00 (.77)	3.13 (.99)	3.39 (.99)	3.38 (1.30)
Grace	3.55 (.93)	2.50 (.93)	3.52 (.73)	3.13 (.83)
Hazel	4.36 (.67)	3.38 (.92)	3.09 (.79)	2.75 (1.58)
Addison	3.91 (.54)	3.75 (.46)	2.48 (.59)	2.63 (.52)
Aurora	4.73 (.47)	4.75 (.46)	2.61 (.99)	3.13 (.83)

Table 4.3 The mean and standard deviation values for the positive and negative emotions during the visits to SL

	LLC	LLE	LLB	LLA
M (SD)	3.86 (1.02)	3.71 (1.11)	2.14 (1.00)	1.92 (1.11)

boredom (LLB) and language learning anxiety (LLA), as well as specific means and standard deviations based on participants' self-ratings indicated in the in-world session logs for the entire sample. As can be seen from these data, the participants were highly curious about learning English in SL (M = 3.86, SD = 1.02) and they highly enjoyed learning the target language in this virtual world (M = 3.71, SD = 1.11). The results also revealed that the students were not particularly bored or anxious while learning English in SL (M = 2.14, SD = 1.00 and M = 1.92, SD = 1.11, respectively).

Self-reported levels of the positive and negative emotions in Group 1, Group 2 and Group 3 in SL

Based on the analysis of the data obtained by means of the LLCS, LLES, BPELC-R and FLCA (see p. 63), the participants were divided into three groups. Group 1 comprised seven students who displayed very high or high levels of the two positive emotions (i.e., language learning curiosity and enjoyment) and neutral or low levels of the two negative emotions (i.e., boredom and language anxiety). Group 2 encompassed six learners who demonstrated a very high or high level of one positive emotion and neutral or low levels of negative and positive emotions. Group 3 included three individuals who exhibited a mixture of high/neutral/low levels of positive and/or negative emotions. First, the self-reported levels of curiosity, enjoyment, boredom and anxiety between the three groups of learners will be provided. This will be followed by the presentation of the differences regarding the self-reported levels of the emotions under investigation within the three groups.

As can be seen in Figure 4.1, which graphically presents the overall levels of self-reported LLC, LLE, LLB and LLA in Group 1, Group 2 and Group 3, and Table 4.4, which provides specific means and standard deviations for these levels, the members of Group 2 reported more curiosity in learning English in SL than their counterparts in Group 1 and Group 3. However, the differences in the means between the three groups were quite small: 0.05 between Group 1 and Group 2, 0.18 between Group 1 and Group 3, and 0.23 between Group 2 and Group 3. As for the positive emotion of enjoyment, the analysis showed that, again, Group 2 scored higher than the other two groups, that is, its members exhibited the most enjoyment in learning English in SL. More specifically, the differences in the means between the three groups were as follows: 0.12 between Group 1 and Group 2, 0.27 between Group 2 and Group 3, and 0.15 between Group 1 and Group 3. When it comes to the experience of boredom, the students in Group 1 turned out to be more likely to succumb to this negative emotion when practicing English in the virtual world than their counterparts in Group 3 and Group 2. The differences in the means were 0.37 between Group 1 and Group 2, 0.20 between Group 1 and Group 3, and 0.17 between Group 2 and Group 3. As far as the negative emotion of language anxiety is concerned, the results revealed that the students in Group 3 and Group 1 felt the most and the least anxious during sessions in SL, respectively. In more specific terms, the difference in the means was 0.10 between Group 1 and Group 2 and 0.49 between Group 2 and Group 3. The largest difference, 0.59, was between Group 1 and Group 3.

Table 4.4 The mean and standard deviation values for self-reported positive and negative emotions in Group 1, Group 2 and Group 3 in SL

	LLC	*LLE*	*LLB*	*LLA*
		M (SD)		
Group 1	3.81 (.58)	3.65 (.75)	2.37 (.64)	1.85 (.57)
Group 2	3.86 (.71)	3.77 (.94)	2.00 (.57)	1.95 (.91)
Group 3	3.63 (1.42)	3.50 (1.18)	2.17 (.65)	2.44 (.71)

66 *Research findings*

Now that the overall self-reported levels of the positive and negative emotions under investigation in the three groups have been discussed, it is time to concentrate on the variation of these emotions observed within each group. As regards Group 1, overall its members self-reported high levels of positive emotions (i.e., language learning curiosity and enjoyment) and low levels of negative emotions (i.e., boredom and language anxiety) – *nota bene* a pattern that turned out to be characteristic of all three groups (see Figure 4.1 and Table 4.4). The differences in the means between the investigated emotions were as follows: 1.44 between curiosity and boredom, 1.96 between curiosity and anxiety, 1.28 between enjoyment and boredom and 1.80 between enjoyment and anxiety. When it comes to Group 2, overall the following differences in the means between positive and negative emotions could be observed: 1.86 between curiosity and boredom, 1.91 between curiosity and anxiety, 1.77 between enjoyment and boredom and 1.82 between enjoyment and anxiety. Finally, in Group 3 the following general differences in the means between positive and negative emotions were found: 1.46 between curiosity and boredom, 1.19 between curiosity and anxiety, 1.33 between enjoyment and boredom and 1.06 between enjoyment and anxiety.

Self-reported levels of the positive and negative emotions for individual learners in SL

While thus far the focus has been on overall patterns either within the entire sample or the three groups that emerged as a result of the initial quantitative analysis, the present section focuses on fluctuations in self-reported levels of LLC, LLE, LLB and LLA from one session in SL to another in the case of individual learners comprising Group 1, Group 2 and Group 3.

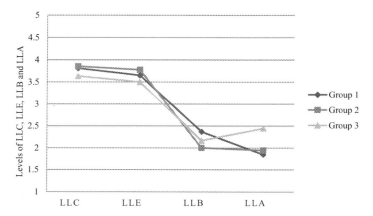

Figure 4.1 Overall levels of self-reported language learning curiosity, enjoyment, boredom and anxiety for each group in SL

Research findings 67

Individual learners comprising Group 1

Table 4.5 and Figure 4.2 present the aggregated self-reported levels of LLC, LLE, LLB and LLA obtained through the in-world session log for individual learners in Group 1. As can be seen from the data and their graphical representation, the general pattern of high levels of positive emotions and low levels of negative emotions that defines the group as a whole was mirrored in the patterns reported by only two (i.e., Aurora and Addison) out of the seven participants. The five remaining subjects, on the whole, experienced various emotions with different levels of intensity, ranging from high to low (e.g., Abigail), from neutral to high and low (e.g., Jack) or from high to neutral, low and very low (e.g., Emma). A very interesting case is Jack, who was the only student to manifest a high level of boredom in this group. It should also be noted that some members of Group 1 manifested considerable individual variation in their self-reported experience of both positive and negative emotions, as evident in the overall standard deviation values (e.g., Aurora).

As can be seen in Figure 4.3, which graphically presents the levels of curiosity, enjoyment, boredom and anxiety reported by individual participants in Group 1 for each session, Aurora was very curious about learning English in SL and she enjoyed it from the initial until the penultimate session (a self-rating of 5 on all occasions except Visit 2 in which her curiosity about learning the TL dropped by one point). The situation changed in the last session, in which the participant lost her curiosity and disliked the study of English (both 2 points). Although the student did not experience a lot of boredom in most of her sessions in SL (from 1 to 2 points in Visits 1–4), she felt extremely bored on Visit 5, which, incidentally, coincides with a drop in curiosity and enjoyment. Aurora felt relatively anxious (3 points) during the first visit, but somewhat less anxious in Visits 2–3 and the learner did not report any feelings of this negative emotion in the last session. Debra reported high levels of curiosity in all but one session in SL (i.e., Visits 1–3 → 4 points, Visit 4 → 3

Table 4.5 The mean and standard deviation values for self-reported levels of language learning curiosity, enjoyment, boredom and anxiety for individual learners in Group 1 in SL

Group 1	LLC	LLE	LLB	LLA
		M (SD)		
Aurora	4.20 (1.30)	4.40 (1.34)	2.20 (1.64)	2.00 (.71)
Debra	3.75 (.50)	4.00 (.00)	2.00 (.00)	1.00 (.00)
Emma	3.88 (.35)	3.38 (.52)	2.25 (.89)	1.13 (.35)
Jack	2.75 (1.50)	3.00 (.82)	3.75 (.96)	2.00 (.00)
David	3.50 (.58)	2.50 (1.29)	2.25 (.50)	2.50 (1.29)
Abigail	4.60 (.55)	4.60 (.55)	1.80 (.45)	2.00 (.00)
Addison	4.00 (1.00)	3.67 (.58)	2.33 (.58)	2.33 (.58)

68 Research findings

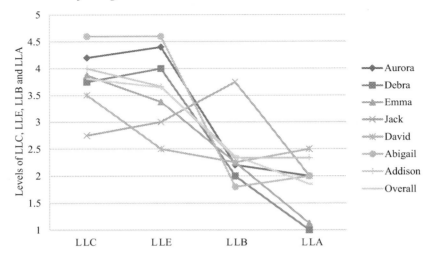

Figure 4.2 Overall self-reported levels of language learning curiosity, enjoyment, boredom and anxiety for individual learners in Group 1 in SL

points) and she also greatly enjoyed learning English there (all visits → 4 points). The student did not feel particularly bored (all visits self-rated at 2 points) and she reported no feelings of anxiety at all in any of the sessions. As for Emma, she was not particularly curious about learning English in the first session (3 points), but subsequently the student's curiosity increased by one point and remained at that level until the last session. It can also be observed that the learner somewhat enjoyed learning English in the virtual world during several sessions (i.e., Visits 1–2 and Visits 5–7) and she highly enjoyed the experience during some others (i.e., Visits 3–4 and Visit 8). Emma felt a bit bored in the first two sessions (2 points each) but she reported no boredom on Visit 3. This was followed by two increases in her experience of this negative emotion (Visit 4 → 1 point, Visit 5 → 4 points) and two decreases in this feeling (Visit 6 → 3 points and Visit 7 → 2 points). The last visit saw no change in the level of boredom, which was low and stood at 2 points. As regards the experience of anxiety, its feeling was reported by Emma only with respect to the initial visit; however, its level was low (2 points). Jack displayed high levels of curiosity about practicing English in SL only in the first two sessions (i.e., Visits 1–2 → 4 points, Visit 3 → 2 points, Visit 4 → 1 point). The student's levels of enjoyment changed from session to session, with Visit 2 and Visit 4 being the most and the least enjoyable (4 and 2 points, respectively). As for the experience of the negative emotions, that is, boredom and language anxiety, Jack felt increasingly more boredom in the last two sessions (Visit 3 → 4 points and Visit 4 → 5 points) when compared to Visit 1 and Visit 2 in which his boredom level stood at 3 points but his feelings of anxiety were low and remained at the same level (i.e., 2 points) from one visit to the

Research findings 69

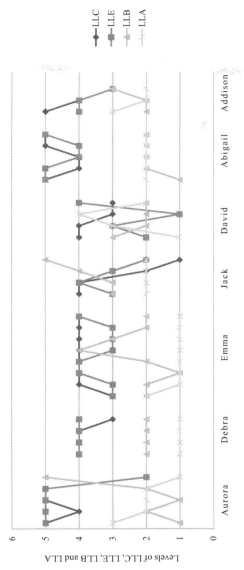

Figure 4.3 Self-reported levels of language learning curiosity, enjoyment, boredom and anxiety in each session in SL: individual learners in Group 1

next. As can be seen in Figure 4.3, David's levels of positive and negative emotions were in a state of flux. The most visible changes in the levels of emotions under investigation concerned language learning enjoyment and anxiety, with the former being the lowest in Visit 3 and the highest in Visit 4 and the latter being the lowest in Visit 1 and highest in Visit 3. David's levels

70   *Research findings*

of curiosity about learning English in SL were higher by one point in the first two sessions when compared to the last two visits. When it comes to the experience of boredom, it turned out to be less susceptible to changes in view of the fact that this negative emotion remained at a low (the same) level during most of the visits. The levels of the positive and negative emotions reported by Abigail did not undergo much variation from one session to another. This is because in the case of the experience of language learning enjoyment and curiosity, a one-point increase and/or decrease could only be observed and in the case of the negative emotions of boredom and language anxiety their intensity remained at the same level (the only exception being the increase by one point in the level of boredom from Visit 1 to Visit 2). Finally, Addison reported shifting levels of the emotions under investigation throughout her adventure with SL, with the largest changes being observed in the student's curiosity about learning English (i.e., a decreasing trend from 5 to 3 points can be observed).

Individual learners comprising Group 2

The analysis of the data gathered by means of the in-world session log revealed that the overall pattern of high levels of positive emotions and low levels of negative emotions observed in Group 2 was distinctive of only one (i.e., Isabella) out of the six participants (see Table 4.6 and Figure 4.4). The remaining students comprising this group reported an amalgam of emotion intensity. More specifically, Ava experienced very high levels of curiosity and enjoyment but very low levels of boredom and language anxiety. Jacob displayed high levels of positive emotions, a low level of boredom and a very low level of language anxiety. Olivia and Hazel both reported neutral levels of language learning curiosity, enjoyment and boredom but low and high levels of language anxiety (Olivia and Hazel, respectively). Finally, Amelia' self-reported general levels of the emotions under investigation represented the most diversified pattern, that is, the learner displayed a very high level of enjoyment in learning English in SL, a high level of curiosity, a very low level of language anxiety and a low level of boredom.

Table 4.6 The mean and standard deviation values for self-reported levels of language learning curiosity, enjoyment, boredom and anxiety for individual learners in Group 2 in SL

Group 2	LLC	LLE	LLB	LLA
		M (SD)		
Ava	5.00 (.00)	4.71 (.49)	1.29 (.49)	1.29 (.76)
Jacob	3.60 (1.14)	3.80 (.84)	2.20 (.45)	1.40 (.89)
Isabella	3.80 (.84)	4.20 (1.30)	1.60 (1.34)	2.20 (1.10)
Olivia	3.40 (.55)	2.60 (.55)	2.60 (.89)	1.80 (1.30)
Hazel	3.00 (1.00)	2.67 (2.08)	2.67 (1.53)	3.67 (2.31)
Amelia	4.33 (.58)	4.67 (.58)	1.67 (.58)	1.33 (.58)

Research findings 71

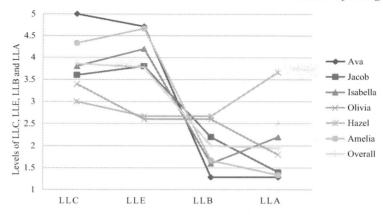

Figure 4.4 Overall self-reported levels of language learning curiosity, enjoyment, boredom and anxiety for individual learners in Group 2 in SL

The changes in the levels of curiosity, enjoyment, boredom and anxiety reported by individual students in Group 2 each time they visited SL are graphically presented in Figure 4.5. The least variation in the levels of the emotions under investigation can be observed in the case of two students, that is, Ava and Amelia. Both students were very curious about learning English and they enjoyed the study of it in SL and at the same time they experienced low or very low levels of boredom and language anxiety from session to session in this virtual environment. More specifically, in most cases, the levels of the positive and negative emotions oscillated between the values of 4 and 5, and 2 and 1, respectively. It should also be noted that in the case of Ava, the experience of curiosity remained on the same and very high level during all her visits to SL and the student's feeling of language anxiety continued to be very low throughout the use of SL, with the exception of only Visit 3, during which this negative feeling reached the value of 3 points. As regards the other students comprising Group 2, more diverse levels of the investigated emotions can be observed (see Figure 4.5). Jacob reported high and very high levels of curiosity in his first two sessions in SL, but then a steady decrease in this emotion could be detected (e.g., Visit 3 → 4 points, Visit 5 → 2 points). Similar to language learning curiosity, the student reported a declining level of enjoyment in learning English from one session in SL to another, with Visit 1 generating the highest (5 points) and the last visit the lowest (3 points) intensity of this emotion. As far as the student's negative emotions of boredom and language anxiety are concerned, they were pretty stable and low (boredom) and very low (anxiety), the only exception being Visit 1 and Visit 2 during which the participant reported a change in the level of his experience of boredom and anxiety (both 3 points). Isabella's level of curiosity was the lowest in the first two sessions and highest during the third visit (3 and 5 points, respectively). The student enjoyed learning English through SL the

72 Research findings

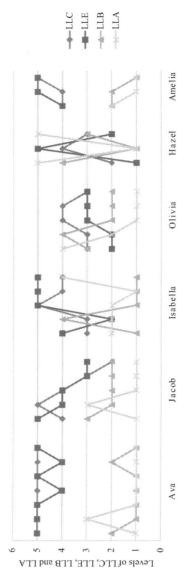

Figure 4.5 Self-reported levels of language learning curiosity, enjoyment, boredom and anxiety in each session in SL: individual learners in Group 2

most during the last three sessions (i.e., Visits 3–5 → all 5 points) but this feeling proved to be the least intense during Visit 2 (2 points). Isabella did not experience boredom in all except one session, that is, Visit 2, in which this aversive feeling skyrocketed and reached the level of 4 points. As for language anxiety, the level of this emotion was low on Visits 1–3, followed by no

Research findings 73

anxiety in Visit 4 and a sudden increase in this negative emotion during the last visit (i.e., 4 points). As can be seen in Figure 4.5, the positive emotions of curiosity and enjoyment in learning English in SL reported by Olivia were relatively stable in view of the fact that only a one-point difference in the self-ratings can be observed between some sessions. For example, in the case of curiosity, a change from 3 to 4 points between Visit 2 and Visit 4 was reported, and in the case of enjoyment, a change from 2 to 3 points between Visit 2 and Visit 3 was detected. Even a cursory look at Figure 4.5 reveals that more dramatic changes occurred in the levels of negative emotions; however, they characterized mainly the student's initial visits to SL. For example, Olivia reported a high level of boredom on Visit 2 but in the following visits the learner's boredom was low (Visits 3–5 → all 3 points). Finally, Hazel's levels of the emotions under investigation were in a state of flux. The participant was the most curious (4 points) and satisfied (5 points) about learning English in SL in Visit 2, but Hazel was the least curious (2 points) and she did not enjoy learning English at all in-world during Visit 1. As for the experience of boredom, the student was the most bored in her initial session but she did not report any feelings of boredom on Visit 2. Hazel experienced the most anxiety in the first and the last sessions but did not feel anxious about learning the target language in SL during Visit 2 (see Figure 4.5).

Individual learners comprising Group 3

The results obtained through the in-world session log demonstrate that the general level of high and low positive and negative emotions, respectively, displayed by Group 3 as a whole was mirrored in the self-ratings of only one student (i.e., Sophia) (see Table 4.7 and Figure 4.6). The other two participants experienced very high (Grace) and low (Gianna) levels of language learning curiosity and enjoyment as well as low (Grace) and neutral (Gianna) levels of boredom and language anxiety.

As graphically presented in Figure 4.7, Gianna was the most and the least curious about learning English in SL during Visit 1 and Visit 3, respectively. In the remainder of the sessions, the student displayed low intensity of the

Table 4.7 The mean and standard deviation values for self-reported levels of language learning curiosity, enjoyment, boredom and anxiety for individual learners in Group 3 in SL

Group 3	LLC	LLE	LLB	LLA
		M (SD)		
Gianna	2.00 (.71)	2.20 (.45)	2.80 (.84)	3.20 (.84)
Sophia	4.40 (.55)	3.80 (.45)	2.20 (1.30)	1.80 (.84)
Grace	4.50 (.55)	4.50 (.55)	1.50 (.55)	2.33 (1.75)

74 *Research findings*

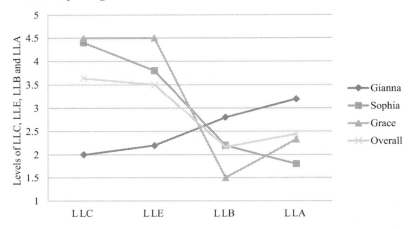

Figure 4.6 Overall self-reported levels of language learning curiosity, enjoyment, boredom and anxiety for individual learners in Group 3 in SL

emotion in question. Gianna displayed a steady and low level of language learning enjoyment throughout her adventure in SL: in all but one session (i.e., Visit 3 – 3 points) the student's self-reported level of this positive emotion was 2 points. When it comes to the negative emotions of boredom and language anxiety, they underwent much more variation from one session to another. For example, Gianna felt the most bored on Visit 3 but the least bored in the last two sessions (i.e., Visits 4 and 5) and the student experienced high levels of language anxiety in the first and the last sessions (both 4 points), but she did not feel very anxious during Visit 3 (2 points). As can be seen in Figure 4.7, Sophia's self-reported levels of curiosity and enjoyment did not undergo much variation and they remained at high or very high levels, with the exception of Visit 1 in which the student self-rated her enjoyment at only 3 points. However, more dramatic changes can be observed in the intensity of the negative emotions under investigation, particularly in the case of boredom. This is because the student experienced high and neutral levels of this aversive emotion during her first two visits to SL but at the same time reported no boredom on Visit 3 and Visit 5. Similarly, although on a smaller scale, changes in the levels of language anxiety can be observed. More specifically, Sophia's experience of language anxiety was on the decrease from her initial visit to SL. As for Grace, her self-reported levels of enjoyment and curiosity about learning English in SL were high and/or very high and they almost went hand in hand from session to session (see Figure 4.7). As regards the experience of boredom, its level remained low and stable (i.e., it oscillated between 1 and 2 points) from the first through the last visit to SL. However, the same cannot be said about the intensity of language anxiety reported by the participant. This is because the experience of this negative emotion underwent substantial changes such as those detected between Visit 1 (1 point) and Visit 2 (4 points) or between Visit 4 (5 points) and Visit 5 (1 point).

Research findings 75

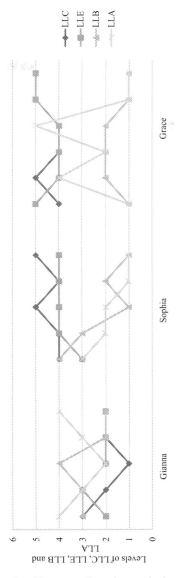

Figure 4.7 Self-reported levels of language learning curiosity, enjoyment, boredom and anxiety in each session in SL: individual learners in Group 3

Qualitative findings

Thus far the focus has been on the levels of the four emotions under investigation within the entire sample, the three groups and individual participants comprising these groups. The present section will be devoted to the

76 Research findings

presentation of the students' emotional accounts of their visits to SL with regard to individual students within Group 1, Group 2 and Group 3.

Participants' emotional accounts of their visits to SL: individual students in Group 1

Aurora

The analysis of the data gathered by means of Aurora's descriptions of her sessions to SL showed that in the first session the student was very curious and excited about the virtual environment in question ("I've played similar games before, but in which all people were speaking Polish," "I didn't know what to expect"). Her feelings of curiosity were high despite the fact that Aurora felt slightly anxious and bored during "a conversation with a man from Brazil"[1] when she had to wait for her interlocutor's replies and who "translated everything [she] said and what he wanted to say." At the same time, Aurora enjoyed this conversation because "some of translated phrases were funny" for her. After this "little chat" the student moved to another location and started a conversation with a girl from Japan. The girl's "English was flawless," which made Aurora anxious, on the one hand, and motivated, on the other, because she "felt the pressure to be correct as well" but had to "try harder" to "choose words more wisely." All in all, Aurora enjoyed talking with the Japanese girl. Aurora described the initial visit to SL as "an adventure without leaving home." The learner enjoyed "the idea of meeting new people from all over the world and learning more about them and their country." Aurora also enjoyed the fact that she "could talk about anything." She remarked:

> During our speaking classes we don't always have an opportunity to talk about our interests or for example the books we like. Here, every topic is worth attention as long as your partner likes it or has something to say about it. Experience with Second Life helped me to estimate the level of my English and it encouraged me to talk more to people online, because it's not as scary as it seems.

When it came to the second session, Aurora and her interlocutors discussed two topics, that is, they chatted about ways of communicating in SL and the users' opinions about this virtual world. Like most of her interlocutors, she preferred text-chatting to having voice-based interactions. She regarded the former as "more comfortable" since, as she said, "when I read the messages I can better understand others and when I write I can think about choosing the right words." Aurora considered her chats in this session as pretty interesting and enjoyable but she also experienced some boredom during some of them. She explained: "Almost all conversations with new people look the same at the beginning, which is normal, but having three conversations in a row in which I need to tell something about myself makes me a bit bored." The student was curious about teleporting to new places in the virtual world and exploring them; however, she found the new spaces "rather small" and thus boring. She wrote: "There are areas that can keep me busy for some time, but they are rather small so when I get to see everything I get bored and start to chat again." The learner summed up her second session in the following way:

> My curiosity level dropped, because I get used to Second Life and the excitement is lower than it was, but I still enjoy it. When it comes to boredom, it's not that easy to decide, because it depends on the conversation I am having. The more I chat the better I feel with my communication skills, so anxiety level is lower than before.

Aurora spent her third session in an art gallery that was opened in a building in SL. She entered the Sky Gallery "curious about the event" and she enjoyed it very much. She admired the works of art and talked to other visitors. The student even attended a party that was thrown in a room "at the top floor" full of dancing people and was instructed how to dance. Needless to say, Aurora did not experience any boredom during this visit; however, she felt somewhat anxious ("My anxiety level was low, but still not on its minimum"). Aurora started her fourth visit to SL with "the traveler who visited Japan many times." As a person who was "passionate about this country," the student asked a lot of questions about Japan. Fortunately for Aurora, her interlocutor "didn't mind [her] curiosity and answered kindly all of them." The participant "felt a little bit anxious" initially but she generally enjoyed the chat and regarded it as "not only pleasant, but also informative." However, the conversation did not last for a long time because Aurora's interlocutor let her know that she "had to go." In her next conversation, Aurora and her new interlocutor discussed life in big cities. The student was curious about the topic, since she "never lived" in a big city but "only visited [one] for some time." The learner did not enjoy the second conversation as much as the first one. She commented: "I was bored after she left, because other conversations were dull."

Aurora described her last session in SL as "rather unfortunate" for her. She wanted to "talk with somebody from Asia," because she was "interested in Japan and its neighbor countries." Unfortunately, as she wrote, "the rumors about Asians not speaking English turned out to be true and I had nobody to talk to there. My previous encounters with English-speaking Asian people were a miracle, I think now. There were so many people and none of them wanted to talk unless it was in their native language." Aurora had no option but to change the location in order to find SL users willing to chat with her. After a number of unsuccessful attempts, Aurora "had a few conversations about [her] country, hobbies, etc. [She] hoped to meet somebody from [her] friend list, but nobody was available. Therefore, [the participant] continued chatting about some mundane topics." The learner summarized the fifth visit in the following words:

78   *Research findings*

This time the curiosity and enjoyment dropped significantly. I wasn't anxious, because I mostly feel anxious when talking to somebody who is on similar or higher language level, but this time I had simple conversations. I think it's the first time I felt so bored in Second Life. Well, everything depends on people we encounter and talk to. This visit wasn't very enjoyable.

Debra

Debra spent the first session in SL together with her classmate. The student "enjoyed teleporting" and was curious about "discovering new places" (e.g., theaters, universities, underwater worlds, beaches or bars). She regarded the visit as "a good occasion to practice speaking in English on many topics." In addition, she wrote: "we managed to keep the flow of our conversation and we were not afraid to correct each other's mistakes in pronunciation or sentence structure." Her self-reported levels of boredom and language anxiety were low or nonexistent since, as Debra explained, "I was talking with my friend so I felt safe." Debra also spent the second visit to SL with her fellow student. The learners talked about a number of topics (e.g., they compared virtual and real worlds, they discussed the current situation in the world related to the spread of the coronavirus and latest news). Similarly to the previous session, the learner enjoyed the visit and was curious about learning English in-world. Moreover, Debra did not report any feelings of anxiety but she "was a bit bored after spending many hours in front of the computer (online classes, doing homework)." During the third session, Debra and her classmate visited the Sky Gallery. The student was curious about the place and she enjoyed talking about a number of exhibits with her classmate as well as dancing. She did not feel anxious but slightly bored at the end of the session. Debra wrote: "I enjoyed this visit but after seeing all of the exhibits and dancing you might get bored because there was nothing else to discover in this place." During the last visit Debra and her classmate discussed the topic related to the differences of living in big cities now and in the past. The learners teleported to "the world of New York City in 1920s–1940s." Debra turned out to be relatively curious about this place; however, her levels of enjoyment, boredom and anxiety did not change when compared to the previous sessions. She commented: "That was something I recognized from old movies. Shops with old-fashioned clothes, old cars, characteristic interior design can be seen everywhere. What drew my attention was plenty of street food and some nice cafes, bars, restaurants located in the ground floor of tenement houses."

Emma

Emma relatively enjoyed her first session in SL. She could meet and talk with a lot of SL users from "every part of the world" in English ("I could talk about different cultures, in my case about India"). The learner experienced some boredom at the beginning of the visit when she felt somewhat lost in the new virtual environment. However, these unpleasant sensations disappeared after a few minutes when Emma got accustomed to this new environment and started to chat with other users ("It became more familiar when I started to have some conversations with others"). The participant enjoyed the possibility of teleporting to different locations within SL and she was curious about different parts of this virtual world ("There is an option to transport to different places. That possibility makes Second Life more interesting and I was curious about where I can go"). Although, due to the avatar she had chosen, Emma did not report much anxiety ("I felt secure because others could not see my real face") and she regarded SL as a good place for practicing English in order to overcome the language barrier ("Second Life is good for learning English when someone has language barrier"); however, she felt a bit anxious in uninhabited places and in situations in which some SL users asked her for personal information. The following excerpt exemplifies this interplay of emotions:

> I was anxious when I transported my avatar to a different location and there was nobody there. The negative thing in Second Life was that some people I wrote with were asking me to give them the name of my Instagram or Facebook account after one minute of talking. It was irritating and I think that younger people who use Second Life could be anxious because of that behavior. I felt anxious and it was uncomfortable.

Emma's second session in SL was dominated by a number of conversations with other users. They discussed "the current situation in the whole world" and "compared Second Life with reality." Emma commented: "The difference is basically that in Second Life we can go out everywhere we want. There is no such possibility in real life because of the budget, and obviously now because of the Coronavirus." Emma also discussed other topics and she was curious about "what other people were saying" but, at times, she experienced some boredom since, as the student expressed: "Not every conversation was great, so I was sometimes bored because people did not know what they were talking about, or they were changing the topic into private questions." Although most of the conversations were interesting, the participant did not enjoy the quality of language produced by some SL residents: "I do not enjoy it when someone writes incorrectly, with sophisticated shortcuts about some stupid things."

In the third session, Emma carried out a few chats with SL residents about the quality of life in this virtual world. This visit was enjoyable for her and she was curious about the possibilities offered by SL to its users, including the study of English. She wrote: "You can simply log into Second Life and enjoy the moment, talk with others ... This aspect that there is the possibility to be resident of some house, or to have a car, intrigued me. It made me more curious about life in Second Life and the way you can practice your language

80   *Research findings*

skills." The learner did not experience any feeling of boredom or language anxiety ("There were also no problems with language, mostly I bumped into people who knew English at a similar level to me").

The levels of curiosity and enjoyment reported by Emma during the fourth visit were similar to the ones in the previous session. The student visited a city and "was really curious about this place and people's opinions about living in big cities." The student enjoyed her conversations and she did not feel anxious at all, since, as she wrote: "When it comes to language, I think that Second Life is a place where you can develop your communication skills, but not language as a foreign language. Many people there have an average level of English, so I did not experience any language anxiety."

According to Emma, the fifth visit "was ordinary." This is because the conversations the learner carried out with her interlocutors were mostly related to "the coronavirus and how this situation with the virus was developing in the whole world." In addition, she felt "a little bit bored because people did not have many ideas" and the "conversations sometimes seemed to be unnatural." Nevertheless, Emma displayed more curiosity than enjoyment during the chats: "I enjoyed the most the fact that I could get to know some interesting facts about particular cultures. Talking with natives is a kind of factor that makes me curious about other countries." Yet again, Emma did not feel anxious during the visit because she did not find it difficult to communicate in English with her interlocutors. She commented: "It's quite easy for me to write with other users in Second Life. I think that we, the students of English Philology, have a good enough level of English to understand others and express ourselves as well."

During the sixth visit Emma was invited by her interlocutors to a new location, that is, a beach. Despite the fact that the chat was successful, and Emma considered it "a good experience that [she] could tell someone about Poland and these persons were fascinated about [her] country," the visit turned out to be "nothing special" for her. The seventh visit was described by Emma as "pretty pleasant." She met new SL users from different countries and they chatted about "schools." Although Emma enjoyed this session, she did not like the fact that several SL users joined the conversation and sent lots of messages ("I was enjoying this session in Second Life despite the fact that it is irritating when you chat with one or two persons and many other people write to you at the same time. It is not possible to answer to all so you have to ignore many people"). As usual, Emma did not feel anxious during the chats. She wrote: "I did not experience any anxiety. Language is not a problem when it comes to Second Life because our generation uses English in various social media such as Instagram. Besides, I'm invisible there." The last session in SL resulted in high levels of her curiosity and enjoyment. Emma chatted with several SL users about learning foreign languages. The following comment illustrates this:

> It was a nice experience to get to know their opinion which languages they like. I was surprised that they told me the Polish language sounds beautiful for them but they are afraid of some sounds that remind them

of snakes. Thanks to these conversations I know what others think about my language. I also shared my opinion about their languages and we had a great conversation because those people wanted to know my feelings too. One could say that it was an interesting time in Second Life that sparked curiosity.

As with the previous sessions, Emma did not experience much boredom and she did not feel anxious at all during the last visit. She commented: "When you talk about something interesting you are not bored or anxious."

Jack

The first session in SL made Jack "feel a little bit curious about this virtual place." During the visit the student "explored part of it and met some interesting people" who besides being regular SL residents, turned out to be students. Jack "felt excited" about chatting with them on a variety of topics; however, as the student put it, "the most enjoyable part was talking about the virus crisis and how we handle this situation." Although the participant did not experience much anxiety throughout the session, he felt somewhat bored with the quality of English produced by his interlocutors. He commented:

Unfortunately, I couldn't learn a lot of new expressions in English because most of the people I tried to talk to used very "primitive" language, I would say. It was obvious they are not really familiar with English and after some time it became boring as communication was hard.

Jack participated in two conversations during his second session in SL. The first one was carried out with two "friendly" students from Georgia. The conversation was enjoyable and beneficial for his TL development. He was also curious to know more about his interlocutors' view on SL. He wrote: "I really enjoyed this conversation because they were really friendly and I learned some new expressions and words. I was curious about their approach to Second Life and what their project is about." As far as the second conversation is concerned, it was conducted with "a weird man from Brazil" who "didn't speak English very well." This fact made this conversation "a little bit boring" for Jack, especially when his interlocutor used "his own expressions and wasn't able to explain what was on his mind."

According to the participant, the third sessions in SL did not "really differ from the previous one." Jack did not meet "any new interesting people ... just old friends" with whom he chatted about "football," their "expectations about the rest of the academic year" and their "feelings during lockdown." Jack felt bored in view of the fact he did not learn any "words and expressions in English" but, simultaneously, the learner was not anxious about using the target language ("I feel free talking there as they can't see my real face and there is no one to judge me").

82   *Research findings*

The last session in SL was "the most boring" for Jack. He did not encounter any "interesting" people who would like to talk with him "for a little bit longer" so he did not learn anything "from the users." Needless to say, the student's levels of curiosity and enjoyment about learning the target language in SL were very low, similar to the level of anxiety.

David

For David the first visit to SL was boring even though he was genuinely curious about this virtual environment. The student did not have the opportunity to practice English during this session due to the fact that his interlocutors' level of English proficiency was low. He commented:

> Learning English was difficult because out of three people with whom I spoke, two were not native English speakers. I met a guy from Brazil and Pakistan that spoke, well, not the highest quality English.

David's experience of boredom was also accompanied by the self-perceived lack of purpose and the feeling of being lost in the virtual world. The student wrote: "I felt boredom when I actually had no idea where to go or what to do. I felt lost there."

The next time David logged in to SL he was more successful. He met a girl who did a "task for her studies in University of Toronto." David felt that he could "learn a lot from" the newly encountered user. The student enjoyed the conversation and was pleased that she liked his English. He remarked:

> This time I enjoyed most of the conversation with a native speaker. She was very impressed with my English, which was shocking for me as I never considered myself as someone who is really good in this language.

All of this made David curious about SL and thus this session did not evoke high feelings of boredom in his case. The student further commented: "I am curious what else this virtual world has to offer. I guess a lot because it is big. I didn't feel bored almost at all this time because I had such a great companion."

Abigail

Abigail considered her initial visit to SL to be enjoyable and entertaining. Although she was a person who was not very computer savvy ("I do not handle technology well"), she did manage to get around the virtual world successfully. She was curious about the opinions of the avatars she had a chance to chat with about "light topics" and these conversations did not result in feelings of boredom or language anxiety, since, as the learner put it: "Nothing made me bored or anxious." The level of enjoyment did not change during the second time Abigail visited SL. During this visit the student teleported to different locations and chatted with randomly met avatars. She noted: "In my opinion this is a very good way to learn English, because I can consolidate main words, learn some new ones and have pleasure when exploring new areas." It should be noted, however, that the learner experienced some boredom due to technical problems, which made her inactive for some time: "What made me bored was that my computer froze from time to time and I had to wait for a long time till it fixed." The third session in SL did not bring about much change. This is because Abigail enjoyed chatting with SL users and she was curious about the possibilities offered by this virtual environment, including those related to learning the target language. The next session (i.e., Visit 4) saw Abigail chatting with her classmates and some fortuitously encountered SL inhabitants. She enjoyed the conversations and felt extremely curious about the "tips" her interlocutors offered her. For example, she wrote: "One of the tips, is the opportunity of gathering money, taking money out of trash cans. The money is needed in order to make full use of what SL has to offer, so I was quite excited after finding out this rather simple way of getting money." The high level of curiosity and enjoyment and low levels of boredom and anxiety were also exhibited by the participant during her last session in SL (i.e., Visit 5). This time Abigail was very curious about the fact that SL users could "be in a relationship" and to hear about SL inhabitants' views on this issue. In fact, the student "met a couple in love" in the course of this visit and chatted with them about their relationship in SL.

Addison

Addison was "quite skeptical" about using SL in order to practice her English skills during the initial session in this virtual world. This is because the student had some experience in utilizing "a similar platform" in the past and she was not pleased with its outcome. She remarked: "I met many people with whom it wasn't pleasant to talk or they wanted to talk about things I wasn't interested in at all." In the course of the second visit to SL, Addison struck up a conversation with "a nice guy" whose "English was quite good enough so [she] also had the opportunity to demonstrate [her] language skills." The student enjoyed chatting with her interlocutor about "a lot of interesting topics" such as the differences and similarities between the real and the virtual worlds. Addison was particularly curious about his experiences related to SL and, although she had just begun her "adventure with the virtual world Second Life," this fact did not stop her "from expressing some of [her] observations on this topic." She was satisfied with the conclusion they reached: "What I liked most was the conclusion we reached together. It was that the virtual world is a place where we can move into our own dreams, create a world only as we like it. But we must be careful that the virtual world does not replace the real world." In the first half of the last visit to SL

84   *Research findings*

Addison tried to chat with many SL users but her attempts were unsuccessful, which induced feelings of boredom and some anxiety. Finally, the student encountered "a girl," who, like her, "was interested in playing instruments, especially the piano and the guitar." Addison enjoyed the conversation and was curious about the girl's views on different topics they discussed. The student commented: "The conversation was nice because her English was quite good. We also talked about the current situation in the world, about how we live in such conditions. We also wrote about the fact that platforms like Second Life are great in these times because we can still stay in touch with people without leaving our homes and with safety rules."

Participants' emotional accounts of their visits to SL: individual students in Group 2

Ava

For Ava, the initial visit to SL was enjoyable and devoid of boredom (although a bit tiring "after using it for two hours straight"). During the visit the student carried out brief chats with SL users she came across randomly while exploring the world, which brought about feelings of curiosity as well. During her second visit, Ava was invited by the encountered SL user to "the part of the world that in his opinion was really worth seeing." She accepted his offer and "followed him after his teleportation request." To her surprise, she arrived at "the building filled with beds" and "saw a bunch of options connected with physical pleasures." Although the visit and the chat with the interlocutor triggered high levels of curiosity and enjoyment in the student, it also sparked a substantial increase in her feeling of anxiety. As for the following session in SL (i.e., Visit 3), it triggered the highest levels of positive emotions in Ava, that is, curiosity and enjoyment, and simultaneously produced no feelings of boredom and language anxiety. This is because she met "amazing people" who told her "a lot about their adventures" in this virtual environment. The participant also learned about her interlocutors' reasons for visiting SL. She noted:

> What frequent visitors like about spending time in Second Life are as follows: meeting people from all around the world and chatting with them; the realism of the world, interaction between people and sharing ideas with them (social aspects of the world). Some people are also interested in the possibility of forgetting about real life – they feel satisfied when they can run away from their problems and are able to do whatever they like. Another comment was that people really appreciate the creativity of the creators and the immensity of the world.

The fourth visit to SL did not bring about much change in Ava's levels of positive and negative emotions, with the exception of her feelings of enjoyment, which were a bit lower. The participant noted: "Despite talking, I also repeated everything that I do every time while being in SL: flying, teleporting to other worlds, discovering interesting places." The following session (i.e., Visit 5) was equally enjoyable and interesting for the participant. During her conversations in the target language with SL residents she heard about the Linden scripting language; however, she did not learn "how to use it." On the sixth visit, Ava continued chatting in English with "the members of the world" and "visiting many new places by teleporting to them." During the conversations she learned about the potential to "get a dog or take a job" or "to organize concerts in Second Life." The student enjoyed the fact that she "could learn some new words thanks to the possibility of chatting with others." The last session in SL (i.e., Visit 7) invariably triggered high levels of positive emotions and low levels of negative emotions. She found out "some interesting facts" about SL concerning, for example, the length of a day in SL, the most important and celebrated days in SL ("the most important day of the year in Second Life is April 1st. The April Fool's day is the most celebrated day").

Jacob

Jacob was pleased with his first session in SL. He "managed to speak via chat in English" with both SL inhabitants and his classmates. He remarked: "that was a very interesting, fresh experience." He was interested in discovering new parts of the virtual world in which he had the opportunity to meet new users. At the end of the session, however, after spending a lot of time in-world, the participant felt tired and started to experience boredom. During the second visit to SL, Jacob chatted with several SL users. During the conversation one of the interlocutors "started making flips in the air," which made the student curious. The learner wanted to learn "the trick" so he started asking questions. However, Jacob's interlocutor turned out to be reticent and the English he produced was incomprehensible. The situation made Jacob anxious and bored. In the course of the next session (i.e., Visit 3), the student saw "many new things." He noted, however, that many of them were "empty" (e.g., "I was in North Korea – an empty place. I saw an empty police car"). He interviewed a number of SL users in order to "find out their aims and reasons" for using SL. It turned out that most of his interlocutors liked SL mainly because they could meet and talk with others, but some of them were annoyed by "the lack of morals." He commented: "real emotions are hidden behind each avatar so some people take advantage of that." Jacob did not experience much boredom during this visit. He was considerably curious about his interlocutors' views and he enjoyed his chats. He admitted, however, that it "was not that easy considering the fact people are not relatively likely to talk with strangers." The remaining two sessions in SL (i.e., Visit 4 and Visit 5) resulted in decreasing levels of curiosity and enjoyment but stable levels of boredom and anxiety. During these two sessions, Jacob "had a

86 *Research findings*

couple of discussions with other users, who talked about some interesting things connected with this virtual world." In the course of the fourth visit, the student found out about the possibility of owning a car and the need to possess a driving license to "play with cars." During the last visit Jacob learned about some facts related to SL. For example, he wrote: "Crimes like stealing can be committed but the penalty is quite serious. If you are caught stealing in Second Life, you can be banned from the game forever."

Isabella

At the beginning of the first visit to SL Isabella "could not find" herself in the virtual world, since, as she put it "I am not really into technology and virtuality." In addition, the initial minutes turned out to be a little anxiety-inducing for the learner because she "couldn't find anybody to talk with." Luckily for Isabella, a SL user approached her and they started to chat. Isabella "enjoyed this small talk a lot" and she "didn't feel any anxiety or boredom." Soon after the conversation ended, the learner "found" her "friend from the group" and they "started talking." Isabella remarked: "it was a casual conversation about what we are doing now and how we cope with the quarantine." Despite the fact that Isabella did not learn anything new during the conversation, she appreciated the opportunity to use English in the unusual setting and feel relaxed. The student commented:

> I am not quite sure if I can say that I have learned English, because we used rather simple vocabulary and our grammar wasn't always correct, but I liked that I wasn't anxious like I often am during the normal classes. I enjoyed the fact that nobody graded or corrected me. It was really useful to practice my language, because now I barely speak English as my parents don't know this language. The time flew past very fast, just like during our conversations in Polish. The most enjoyable thing for me was that I could pretend that I am on a walk or having coffee with my friend.

The subsequent session in SL (i.e., Visit 2) was very boring and not enjoyable for Isabella ("This time in Second Life was boring, and I did not have many chances to talk to other people"). The participant had problems with finding SL users willing to chat with her ("There were fewer people than before, and I had to focus more on finding other users than talking"). In addition, most of the SL users she managed to interact with "didn't speak English very well" so she "was really bothered by mistakes that they made." Isabella's attempts to find her classmate with whom she had chatted in the previous session also came to nothing. When the student finally "found other avatars ready to talk to" her, they soon "had to go, or [she] simply lost them in the world, because they teleported somewhere else."

The third session in SL proved to be the opposite of the previous one. Isabella reported a low level of anxiety but no feelings of boredom. Her levels of curiosity and enjoyment were the highest and reached their maximum since she started availing herself of the opportunities offered by the virtual world. Pretending to be a journalist, the student "interviewed" a number of SL inhabitants. She learned about their opinions about SL and some positive aspects of living in this virtual world; however, Isabella heard about some disturbing facts as well. She wrote:

> I met some people who had met there their current best friends. Now, they mainly communicate on Facebook or via e-mail, but they are still visiting Second Life in search of new friendships. Other people told me that they use this platform to socialize with others during the quarantine. One girl told me that she is trying to improve her English and Second Life is a great place to freely communicate with native speakers. I met also people who didn't like talking with others because of some stalkers or people who want to talk about sex. They think that there should be some kind of protection from such people, because also kids use this platform. Personally, I agree with that opinion, because sometimes even the nickname of such a person suggests what is her/his purpose.

Similar to Visit 3, Visit 4 was highly enjoyable and pretty interesting for the learner. Although she met only one SL user, they "surprisingly had many things to talk about." Their "chit-chat" lasted "more than one hour" and they chatted "about everything: about siblings, hobbies, friends and how we perceive other users." Isabella did not experience any boredom or anxiety, since, as she pointed out, "this person had much more advanced level of English than people I had talked to earlier and he only saw my avatar." In the last session (i.e., Visit 5), Isabella continued talking with the person she met during Visit 4. Due to "the broken keyboard" in the participant's laptop, she was forced to "actually talk," which turned out to be "much more stressful that just writing in English." In the end, Isabella managed to "overcome" her anxiety and the conversation was a success. She noted: "I had the chance to talk with somebody at my age in English and that was really good for me, because I do not have many opportunities to use English in my everyday life. So it was really good to finally talk with someone in English."

Olivia

Olivia "felt a little bored" in the initial minutes of her first session in SL since "there was nothing going on and nobody wanted to talk to" her. Therefore, the student decided to "explore the island more and meet some people." The SL users she encountered were "okay but the conversations weren't interesting." After a few rounds of chats, Olivia "met a man from Turkey" and they began to chat about "basic stuff." The student "was impressed by his English" and also "wanted to show [her] English skills." They chatted "for almost an hour" but Olivia felt anxious at the end of their conversation when it

88   *Research findings*

"started getting really weird" so Olivia finished the chat. She commented: "He asked me a lot of indecent questions and I left the chat." Olivia described her subsequent session in SL (i.e., Visit 2) as boring in view of the fact that she could not find SL users who would be willing to chat with her: "Today's adventure with Second Life was a little bit boring. People that I met, didn't really want to talk with me. Nothing spectacular happened today." As a result, the short conversations she managed to carry out with the avatars she encountered were not enjoyable, but they also did not bring about feelings of anxiety ("I wasn't anxious this time because nobody was insistent"). The third visit to SL saw an increase in Olivia's self-reported levels of curiosity and enjoyment but a decrease in her experience of boredom and language anxiety. The student had a chat with "a boy and a girl about their feelings about Second Life." Although Olivia considered herself as a "very skeptical person about the use of computers for communication," she was pleased "to know that for some people, it is a place where they can be themselves." She wrote:

> Both of them agreed that Second Life is an escape for them. They like spending time there because nobody judges them because of their looks and views. They told me that they have had a few unpleasant situations in this virtual world but they have learnt how to avoid them. They met a lot of people there and they still have good contact with them. The boy was bullied in his school and in Second Life he met his "true, virtual" friends. He feels safer in Second Life than in his real life. He finally has friends that understand him.

The levels of positive and negative emotions reported by Olivia remained the same in the course of the fourth visit. Although the learner did not communicate with anyone on this occasion, the levels of positive and negative emotions reported by Olivia remained the same as during the third session. The student described the visit in the following way:

> When I got to the 1920s–1940s New York, the first difference was the vibe. Old cars on the street and the music made me feel like I was really there. There were lots of small shops. I saw how women used to dress and I really liked the fashion exhibition. There were no fancy, big skyscrapers but lovely tenement houses with shops. Everything was kept in brown and gray colors. A big difference I saw in a bar. There were some tables and portraits of people, and of course a piano. Live music in bars was a foundation of those times. Nowadays, people enjoy modern bars and restaurants; I think most of them don't have this unique atmosphere that bars used to have.

The last session in SL "was not boring but was not exciting either" for Olivia. The student "talked with some random people" but she was relatively interested and curious about "the Covid situation" in Italy and Turkey. During the visit Olivia had a chance to practice English. She offered the following comment:

One girl who lives in Italy told me that the situation is getting better. She could finally leave the house for a walk after a few months of isolations. On the other hand, a boy from Turkey said that only the big cities were shut down and in many small towns everything was rather normal. His English was okay but I think he didn't understand some of my words and I had to write basic words. I was a little frustrated about that. I didn't feel anxious. I talked with this girl for an hour, I understood everything. I had to check some words she had written so I learnt something new thanks to her!

Hazel

Hazel did not regard SL as enjoyable in any way and she was not particularly curious about learning English in this environment during her first session. As someone who was "not a big fan of that kind of games," the student felt "confused" and found SL "hard to understand how to use." Her interest in this virtual environment did not change even after Hazel started to comprehend basic functions concerning SL. She wrote: "when I understood how to play it was pretty easy, but still not very interesting." Hazel met a number of SL residents who expressed their eagerness to chat with her; however, most of them turned out to be impolite or simply "rude." Although Hazel liked the fact that she did not see her interlocutors ("We didn't see our faces, only our avatars"), she complained about the output produced by her conversation partners ("sometimes their English level was pretty low") and felt bored. The student also felt uncomfortable and she experienced high levels of anxiety during chats with SL users who "asked about very private things."

The next session in SL (i.e., Visit 2) stood in sharp contrast to the first session. This is because the student's levels of enjoyment and curiosity were high (5 and 4 points, respectively) and she did not report any feelings of boredom or language anxiety. Hazel asked her friend, whom she had known for several years, to meet in SL and spent time talking to her throughout the entire visit:

> I asked my friend to have a full English conversation with me. It was definitely better than looking for somebody there. She finished university 2 years ago, and her dad has been living in London for 10 years. She visits him quite often, so her English level is very high. I have never tried to have a conversation with her in English.

Hazel was "really curious how I will feel about it" and "hear ourselves in English." The two friends talked "about many things, about quarantine, the plans for next few days." Hazel was not "bored at all" since, as she put it, the conversation looked "totally different when you talk with your friend and different when you have to start a conversation with a stranger." Despite the fact that Hazel did not understand everything, she felt comfortable and relaxed during the conversation. In one such situation when the student had

Research findings

difficulty in comprehending a question, she made use of an additional mode of communication, that is, the text chat. She remarked: "There was a moment when I didn't understand her. She asked me a question and I didn't know what to say. But I asked her to write a question in other words, and then everything was clear." Hazel recapped the visit in question in the following way: "I absolutely enjoyed learning English by voice conversation. I felt safe, so I could pay all my attention to a conversation."

Unfortunately for Hazel, her last session in SL (i.e., Visit 3) was similar to the first visit: the student did not enjoy it, she was relatively curious about learning English during it, she felt extremely anxious and fairly bored. Such self-reported levels of the positive and negative emotions were the result of the chats Hazel carried out with impolite SL users who, as the learner wrote, "started to give me more unsuitable questions" and she had to "close the chats."

Amelia

Even though some of Amelia's interlocutors "barely knew English," the student reported high levels of curiosity and enjoyment about practicing the target language during her first session in SL. She was content when she could express her "points of view and they did the same." Amelia, generally, "felt OK when talking with people and it was nice and relaxing" except for one chat the student contemplated joining when she teleported to one of the parts of SL. Amelia did not participate in the chat and moved to a different part of SL when she realized that "the people there were talking about sex and unacceptable topics." The learner experienced some boredom but this feeling was related to technical issues ("I felt boredom because my character was walking very slowly") rather than problems concerning the practice of English. This is not to say, however, than Amelia did not enjoy simply being in SL and taking advantage of some of its potentials: "I enjoyed the most the ability to fly, it was fun." As far as the second session in SL is concerned, Amelia was "satisfied with the visit and conversations [she] had. [She] enjoyed learning English during this visit especially with Sophia." Her interlocutor, Sophia, was 25 years old and lived in the United Kingdom. Amelia "was talking with her almost 1h about books and films we recommend" and "about living in cities." During the session in question Amelia also met "a lot of people" with whom she "talked about the present situation and coronavirus" when they "were not interested in talking about cities." In the third and last session in SL, Amelia "spent [her] time exploring new places rather than talking to people." The participant "was amazed" at the visit. She discovered "a lot of beautiful places" but what she "liked the most was a castle." Amelia said: "I got lost a few times at that castle but it was fun. I met there a strange guy who was talking about ghosts."

Research findings 91

Participants' emotional accounts of their visits to SL: individual students in Group 3

Gianna

Gianna displayed neutral levels of curiosity and boredom, a low level of enjoyment and a high level of language anxiety in the first session in SL. Initially the student was curious about the people she could encounter in-world but soon she became a bit disappointed and bored when she was not able to find and talk with someone the same age as she was. As a person who prefers to communicate in a traditional, face-to-face, manner, Gianna did not feel relaxed when faced with the electronic way of exchanging information characteristic of virtual worlds. In addition, the participant experienced some technical issues related to access to the internet. Gianna remarked:

> I was curious about the people I can meet. To my surprise sometimes it was really hard to find someone close to my age … Unfortunately, after some time I got a little bit bored. I usually do not feel comfortable speaking to someone on the internet (that is because I can't see a person's face) and even though I had met nice people it was hard for me to talk freely. Additionally during the whole time I had a one big problem. I use a mobile internet which means that the data is limited. The game takes a lot of data to open and requires a good, stable connection. A few times it was really hard for me to load it and even if I managed to I could not move so I was forced to re-open it quite often.

The second session in SL did not make Gianna curious about learning the target language. In fact, she regarded the visit as relatively boring, yet she enjoyed it a little more when compared to the first session ("This time I felt more comfortable, however still a little bit boring"). Despite the fact that online communication makes Gianna uncomfortable, she managed to have a pleasant conversation with a friendly stranger and she chatted with her groupmates in English. The learner wrote:

> My main problem is the fact that I am still afraid to talk openly with strangers online. To my surprise I met a really lovely girl and we were talking for a long time. I also met my classmates and talked with them only in English and I must admit that it was a nice experience.

Even though Gianna did not enjoy her third encounter with SL, she was not curious about learning English in-world and reported a lot of boredom, the session in question turned out to be the least stressful for her (she self-reported her level of anxiety at only 2 points). This is because the student tried to overcome her weakness related to the in-world mode of

92 Research findings

communication and, perhaps most importantly, regarded SL as "a nice and useful tool to practice English." Gianna commented:

> With every visit I work on my language barrier and I have to admit that I got more confident in using English online. However, I am still afraid of making some stupid simple mistakes, but I will keep working on that. I also sometimes feel really anxious about talking to people with strange accents or those who are much older than me.

In the subsequent visit to SL (i.e., Visit 4), Gianna felt somewhat more curiosity about the study of English, even if its level was still low, and found it slightly more enjoyable when compared to her last session in this virtual environment. She wrote:

> I need to admit that I entered the world of Second Life just out of the curiosity to talk with my new online friends from all around the world. I also tried to meet new ones. Some people shared their identity and used English fluently without any problems and some didn't. Even though I have no idea who these people in SL are in real life, it is certainly nice to talk with them and practice the language.

While the student has "never been the biggest fan of these kinds of activities especially when it comes to the use of English online," she considered the virtual world SL "actually less a game than an experiment in making [herself] more open to random and unknown people." Yet Gianna kept experiencing language anxiety particularly in situations when she "met and talked to some creepy people." Fortunately, the student learned that "the best way [was] to ignore them."

The last session in SL (i.e., Visit 5) did not bring about much change when it comes to the self-reported levels of the emotions under investigation. Although with reservations, Gianna appreciated the fact that SL made it possible for her "to spend some time together with friends and actually practice the language ... meet people with shared interest" even if, as the student remarked, "sometimes talking with them might be hard due to the time zones." In addition, the visit in question made Gianna realize that she had improved her language skills. She wrote: "I think that my English keeps getting better and better." During the visit Gianna experienced "some boredom" and high anxiety due to her personality and the annoying behavior of some of her interlocutors and SL users she encountered, respectively. She commented:

> I experienced some boredom as I am not really a talkative person and I am not able to focus on a conversation online ... I met and talked with some people who were really annoying because the only thing they cared about was to say inappropriate things.

Research findings   93

Sophia

In the opening visit to the virtual world SL, Sophia felt very curious about "the destinations and an opportunity to meet someone as well as the possibility to communicate in English." The learner relatively enjoyed the visit during which she could "hone" her language skills, since, as she explained, "there is a daily use of English, so I can practice my language on a daily basis." Also, the student liked the fact that she could "decide about [her] appearance." However, Sophia's self-reported level of boredom was high. The experience of this aversive emotion was mostly related to the world's limitations as well as hardware requirements. Equally important was the fact that the participant did not regard herself as a "game fan" and she lacked relevant skills. She remarked:

> Sometimes it was boring because it takes a lot of time to move – especially walking takes a lot of time. The game sometimes doesn't work properly but it is caused by my laptop – it's too poor. To be honest after 20 minutes I was a bit bored. I am not a game fan and it's my first game that I have been playing, so I am inexperienced in the virtual world.

In addition, while exploring this virtual environment during the initial session, meeting a variety of SL users and carrying out occasional chats with some of them, Sophia experienced heightened anxiety. The feelings of this negative emotion were, on the one hand, triggered by visiting some "inappropriate places" in which she found "dirty content" and, on the other hand, chatting with "very rude and indecent people."

The following session in SL (i.e., Visit 2) saw high self-reported levels of enjoyment and curiosity about learning English. This is because Sophia had a few successful conversations with encountered interlocutors about a number of topics. Sophia was pleased with the fact that she could "hone [her] English skills" again. Besides language benefits, the student also learned how to "modify [her] avatar so now the game [gave her] more pleasure." Sophia's self-reported level of language anxiety was low, since, as she explained "I felt secure behind my avatar." However, the learner occasionally experienced the feeling of boredom due to lack of ideas of what to do in the session in question. She offered the following comment: "Sometimes I get bored because I don't have a clear aim and I have to look for it on my own."

In the course of the third visit Sophia reported no feelings of boredom, nor was she particularly anxious. Instead, the student was very highly curious about the new places she visited and what her interlocutors were talking about: She wrote:

> I have met many interesting people. All of them were totally different. They lived and worked in various places. I met even a man who is 60 years old. I also visited a lot of new destinations including London City,

94   *Research findings*

and I discovered new shopping malls. This time the whole experience wasn't boring at all. Although I came across some "odd" residents, they weren't very intrusive so I wasn't very anxious.

Sophia's levels of curiosity and enjoyment were high in the subsequent session in SL (i.e., Visit 4). The student teleported to "the world of Art," in which she "met some people who were interested in art," she "could write with them about their passions," which "made [her] very curious." For Sophia, the visit to the gallery was "a great occasion to use vocabulary connected with art that [she does not] use on a daily basis." The learner did not experience any anxiety while interacting with SL users since, as she wrote: "The fact that I haven't met any rude users makes me happy … it was a pleasant visit to an unknown world which was full of interesting people."

After a two-week break from using SL (due to the student's "lack of time"), Sophia felt "really relaxed" in her last session (i.e., Visit 5) in this virtual environment. The learner "met some new people" with whom she chatted about "different stuff than university, political issues and Coronavirus." Sophia "missed such noncommittal talks" so she was curious about other "people's opinions on the subjects." In addition, Sophia felt "curious about new places" and also "visited some of them." The student remarked: "I found a new shopping mall and changed my avatar. I like the fact that Second Life allows me to be creative and doesn't limit my options regarding appearance."

Grace

Grace was highly enthusiastic about her first visit to SL. Her high self-reported levels of curiosity and enjoyment stood in stark contrast to her self-reported experience of boredom and language anxiety, with the former being by far more intense (four and five points vs. one and one points, respectively). Grace wanted to explore the virtual world and meet people with whom she could interact in English, especially during the time of the spread of the virus (Covid-19) and the lockdown when she had limited occasions to socialize with her peers. She commented:

> It was really interesting to participate in the activity like that. It was really fun time for me. I felt really curious about what am I going to explore, and what am I going to find in this virtual world. I did not experience any boredom or language anxiety. I was sure that my English is not so bad to be afraid of it, or to just feel unsure. I was excited to get to know people and explore new places. I think what I enjoyed the most was just talking to different people, and getting to know them, or just trying to find somebody from my group. I also enjoyed the possibility to meet people during the quarantine and it was really relieving. I don't think that any of the things in Second Life made me bored. I did not feel anxious at all while being in this virtual world. I really enjoyed spending time there.

Research findings 95

Grace continued to enjoy using SL in her second visit to this virtual environment and she felt highly curious about her interlocutors' views on the discussed topics ("I was very interested in their opinions and what they had to offer"). This time, however, she also experienced a sudden burst of high anxiety at the end of the visit in question. This negative feeling was triggered by the fact that Grace "got lost in one part of the world and didn't know how to get out." In order to "get out of" this unexpected and somewhat inopportune situation, the student started to look for SL users who could "show the way"; however, the learner had problems with verbalizing her predicament. She commented: "Suddenly I felt a lot of anxiety, but after a few moments I found out that there is nothing to be afraid of, because there are people who will help you. I felt really good after I logged off, and I had a feeling that we are all connected in at least this world."

In the course of the third and the fourth sessions in SL, Grace reported the same, high levels of curiosity and enjoyment as well as low levels of boredom. Throughout Visit 3 the student pretended to be a journalist and interviewed a great number of SL users about SL. She "had fun" and was curious about the interviewees' opinions about the world in question. She felt "secure behind [her] avatar" even when she approached "rude" SL residents. As for Visit 4, Grace "cheerfully talked" with several SL residents and the learner also found her "friend in here from group." When the two girls "got apart," a SL user approached Grace and they began chatting. The participant was very interested in the conversation; however, she was "not able to understand everything." When they started to discuss a different topic, Grace had problems with conveying her thoughts and she "lacked specific words needed for the topic." As a result, Grace experienced increased anxiety.

During Visit 5 and Visit 6 the student reported very high levels of curiosity and enjoyment and no feelings of boredom or language anxiety. During both sessions Grace met with her friend. They "walked around" and chatted "about casual things." Although "nothing besides it happened," the learner said that "it was fun." Grace summarized the two visits in a similar way: "I felt relaxed and my mind was clear. It was a really nice experience, we were talking for an hour and a half, I didn't notice when that time passed."

Discussion

As will be recalled from Chapter 3, the present research project was intended to explore the positive emotions of curiosity and enjoyment as well as the negative emotions of boredom and anxiety experienced by Polish university students majoring in English during their visits to SL. Before the discussion of the findings is undertaken, it is important to emphasize three important issues at this juncture. First, the visits were informal in nature in the sense that they did not take place during the online classes imposed by the Covid-19 pandemic, nor were they required by the teacher, which is well reflected in the fact that the number of such visits differed from one participant to

96 Research findings

another. Second, the bulk of the analyses were conducted with respect to three distinct student profiles that were determined based on their responses to the questionnaires tapping into the four emotions under investigation, and it should be kept in mind that as such they may have referred mainly to general learning of English in different contexts (including online learning, which was predominant because of the pandemic) rather than to the occurrence of such emotions in virtual worlds. Third, taking into account the innovative nature of this study, which is evident in the fact that it looked in a situated manner into a constellation of positive and negative emotions that has not yet been examined in any setting, it is not always possible to relate the findings to the existing empirical evidence, with the effect that both more general investigations into emotions need to be adopted as a point of reference as well as the authors' intimate knowledge of the context in which this study was undertaken. With these caveats in mind, the five research questions posed for this study can be addressed in the following subsections, which will be followed by a discussion of the limitations of the research project.

RQ1: What levels of the positive (i.e., curiosity and enjoyment) and negative (i.e., boredom and anxiety) emotions do students report and what distinct student profiles can be identified on this basis?

The average responses to the four instruments (i.e., the LLCS, LLES, BPELC-R and FLCA scales) employed in the present study to tap into the four emotions as they are experienced in learning English as a foreign language in general allowed a composite picture of the entire sample as well as providing a basis for profiling participants into three distinct groups. To be more precise, on the whole, the participants reported a high level of positive emotions, with the caveat that the effect of curiosity was much more pronounced than that of enjoyment (4.02 vs. 3.51 on a five-point Likert-scale), whereas the contribution of the negative emotions of boredom and anxiety proved to be comparable and largely moderate (cf. Wattana, 2013). It would thus appear that the process of learning English in the BA program in which the students were enrolled produced a level of novelty that was by and large appropriately pitched, which may have led to optimal arousal (cf. Spielberger & Starr, 1994) and it may have also encouraged participants to actively take steps to satisfy their yearning for new information concerning the TL (cf. Grossnickle, 2016; Litman, 2005; Loewenstein, 1994). Logically, as has been explained by Mahmoodzadeh and Khajavy (2019), this could have triggered the drive to use English for communicative purposes as often as possible, but also to constantly find out more about how the TL works, thus reflecting both L2 communicative curiosity, stemming from a feeling of interest, as well as linguistic curiosity, deriving from the feeling of deprivation. What is unclear is whether this situation is a reflection of the nature of the classes comprising the intensive English course that the students had to attend and the related assignments, the things they did of their own accord to enhance their mastery of the TL, or perhaps some kind of combination of both. In light of the fact that curiosity, at least of the I-type (Litman, 2010) or that which is brought about by communicative interactions (Mahmoodzadeh & Khajavy, 2019), is closely related to enjoyment, it is unsurprising that the intensity of this positive emotion was also quite high. However, it should not escape our attention that the reported level of enjoyment was considerably lower than that of curiosity and it was, in fact, at the upper threshold of the moderate level (Wattana, 2013). One possible explanation for this could be that while language curiosity may have been more stable in the case of the participants who were English majors, perhaps representing more of a trait attribute (Grossnickle, 2016), the feeling of enjoyment was much more dependent on what transpired in the classroom over which the students often did not have sufficient control. As a result, it could be hypothesized that different dimensions of enjoyment may have manifested themselves to different degrees. More specifically, private enjoyment could have been easier to achieve than social enjoyment (Dewaele & MacIntyre, 2016), or, to use the categorization offered by Li et al. (2018), it might have played a more important role than the enjoyment related to the teacher or the classroom atmosphere. Unfortunately, the analysis of specific items included in the LLE scale cannot corroborate or disprove such an interpretation because items belonging to different dimensions were among those with the highest and lowest rankings. The moderate, or what Wattana (2013) labels neutral, levels of boredom and anxiety were to some extent to be expected given the high levels of the positive emotions of curiosity and enjoyment. After all, while the relationships among all of those variables have not been investigated, research in both traditional and CALL settings indicates that enjoyment is on the whole negatively related to anxiety, both at a particular point in time as well as over time, while the levels of boredom and anxiety often go hand in hand (Dewaele & Dewaele, 2020; Dewaele & MacIntyre, 2014; Elahi Shirvan & Taherian, 2021; Kruk, 2019, 2021b; Resnik & Dewaele, 2021). Anyway, it is fair to say that the impact of the negative emotion of boredom, whether understood in terms of disengagement, monotony and repetitiveness, or lack of satisfaction and challenge (Pawlak et al., 2020b) did not overall constitute a major problem for the sample and overall the same can be said about the debilitating effects of foreign language anxiety (Ellis, 2008; Scovel, 1978). Perhaps the existence of this specific constellation of positive and negative emotions can reasonably be attributed to the characteristics of the sample selected for the investigation. This is because it can reasonably be assumed that individuals who had consciously decided to study English to achieve a very high level of proficiency and to become professionals with respect to the use of this language should exhibit high levels of curiosity about different aspects of the TL and on the whole enjoy learning it, even if some aspects of this process can be boredom-inducing or anxiety-provoking.

Detailed analysis of the participants' responses to the four scales tapping into positive and negative emotions allowed identification of three distinct

98   *Research findings*

student profiles that could be further investigated with respect to the emotional reactions triggered by visits to the virtual world. These profiles were as follows: (1) students who manifested very high or high levels of two positive emotions and neutral or low levels of two negative emotions, (2) students who reported a very high or high level of one positive emotion and at the same time manifested neutral or low levels of negative and positive emotions, and (3) students who exhibited a combination of high, neutral and low levels of different kinds of emotions, both positive and negative. Importantly, even in Group 1 and Group 2, there existed individual variation in relation to the reported level of the emotions under investigation (e.g., very high vs. high level of curiosity, neutral vs. low level of boredom and anxiety). Identification of these three profiles is important for two reasons. First, previous research has clearly demonstrated that the emotional trajectories of individual learners tend to deviate considerably from the established group patterns, not least because their distinct, more enduring characteristics (e.g., attitudes, general proneness to boredom, learning styles) produce different emotional reactions to what transpires in the classroom (e.g., Dewaele & Dewaele, 2020; Kruk et al., 2021; Pawlak et al., 2020c). Second, it was believed that the awareness of these profiles would allow the researchers to better categorize and understand the emotional reactions that the participants of the study experienced when visiting the virtual world of SL.

RQ2: What are the overall levels of the positive and negative emotions experienced by the participants in SL?

As explained in Chapter 3, the levels of the positive and negative emotions under investigation were tapped into by means of the participants' self-ratings of these emotions during each visit to SL using a scale of 1 to 5, identical to that used in the questionnaires used to measure general levels of curiosity, enjoyment, boredom and anxiety. When we examine the average reported intensity over the different visits, two parallel trends immediately become visible: first, although the self-ratings of curiosity and enjoyment are still high, the gap between them is much smaller in comparison to the general levels discussed above (3.86 vs. 3.71), which is due to a slight decrease in the former and an equally slight increase in the latter; second; the negative emotions of boredom and anxiety are now in the low range (2.14 and 1.92), with the former somewhat exceeding the latter, which is the reverse of the situation revealed for the data collected by means of the LLCS, LLES, BPELC-R and FLCA. Another interesting difference between the two sets of data, that is, those pertaining to overall levels of the emotions and those reported for visits to SL, is that there was considerably more individual variation in the latter case, as evident in the fact that the standard deviation values were roughly twice as high. Interestingly, the minute and negligible differences in means notwithstanding, identical patterns were detected in Group 1 and Group 2 (see the discussion above). However, this was not the case in Group 3, where the levels of anxiety were considerably higher and they in fact exceeded those of

Research findings 99

boredom. It was also in this group, where the participants reported an amalgam of different emotions of varying intensity, that individual variation was the highest in the case of the two positive emotions (i.e., curiosity and enjoyment).

One plausible interpretation of these results that immediately springs to mind is that it was the opportunity to learn English informally in a virtual world that accounted for the overall more positive emotional reactions than those reported for learning English in general. Although language learning curiosity may have somewhat decreased in intensity, perhaps due to the fact that its communicative facet (Mahmoodzadeh & Khajavy, 2019) could not always be fully exploited (see below for the discussion of factors generating the emotions under investigation), there was an increase in levels of enjoyment, which can reasonably be attributed to the fact that its social dimension or those contingent on the teacher and the overall atmosphere (Dewaele & MacIntyre, 2016; Li et al., 2020) are basically irrelevant under such circumstances. On the other end of the spectrum, it is clear that when participants were given freedom as to when, how and with whom to practice the TL in the virtual environment, they were less likely to succumb to boredom and to suffer the negative effects of anxiety, all the more so as no teacher evaluation was involved in this case. More generally, it might also be not much of a stretch to assume that the advantageous make-up of the positive and negative emotions during visits to SL can be related to the fact that the students could exercise autonomy in the virtual environment, being able to exert control over various facets of the learning process (cf. Benson, 2011; Goodwin-Jones, 2019). These findings are to a large extent in line with existing empirical evidence that shows that the use of technology and in particular online environments are likely to increase positive emotions such as enjoyment (e.g., Lai et al., 2015; Yoshida, 2020a) and reduce negative emotions such as anxiety (e.g., Kruk, 2016c; Lee & Hsieh, 2019; Melchor-Couto, 2017), although we should not forget that prolonged periods of online learning can make it less enjoyable than traditional, face-to-face instruction (cf. Resnik & Dewaele, 2021).

This said, three crucial caveats are in order. First, the considerable individual variation in the experience of positive and negative emotions in SL may suggest that the propitious emotional make-up identified for the whole sample may not hold for everyone. This can be the outcome of an intricate interplay of individual difference (ID) variables (e.g., grit, learning styles, learning strategies, beliefs) that may predispose learners to respond in disparate ways to different online environments as well as the learning opportunities they offer. The case of Jack, whose level of boredom was considerably higher than the other members of Group 1, or Hazel, who was much more anxious than other participants in Group 2, clearly testify to this reality. Second, and closely related to the previous point, when the intensity of emotions is particularly volatile and unpredictable, as was the case with the students in Group 3, the situation becomes much more complex, and although positive emotions may still get the upper hand, little can be taken for granted, particularly in situations when participants are less experienced in learning the TL and represent lower levels of proficiency.

100 *Research findings*

RQ3: How do the levels of positive and negative emotions change from one visit to SL to the next?

Since the groups representing the three distinct student profiles contained different numbers of participants, sometimes very small (e.g., just three students in Group 3) and the number of visits to SL varied among those participants, it made little sense to analyze the averages of the positive and negative emotions for each reported session. For this reason, the discussion of RQ3 as well as RQ4 is based on the trajectories of curiosity, enjoyment, boredom and anxiety, as reported by individual students in each of the three groups. Such analysis demonstrated that, as stipulated by the proponents of complex dynamic systems theories (Larsen-Freeman & Cameron, 2008), the levels of the positive and negative emotions in question were characterized by both change and stability (cf. Hiver et al., 2021), with such patterns being contingent on several factors. For one thing, as shown in the graphical representations in Figures 4.3, 4.5 and 4.7, corresponding to the students' profiles in each group, the fluctuations in the levels of positive emotions proved to be the least evident for students in Group 1, followed by those in Group 2 and Group 3. It would thus appear that the positive emotions of curiosity and enjoyment tended to remain more stable from one session to the next than the negative emotions of boredom and anxiety. Second, close inspection of the trajectories of all the emotions for individual students largely confirms this assumption. This is because, despite some inevitable inter-group and within-group variation, the intensity of positive emotions in all groups tended to be less susceptible to change than that of negative emotions. This said, since the levels of positive emotions were generally high and the levels of negative emotions were generally low, it is not surprising that the former were more likely to decrease and the latter to increase, but the changes in the intensity of curiosity and enjoyment were on the whole of lesser magnitude. This certainly provides food for thought in terms of pedagogical interventions, but it could tentatively be argued that tasks and activities that arouse curiosity and enjoyment are key to effectively managing the emotional climate of online L2 learning. Third, while tendencies of this kind are interesting and quite well visible in the data, they seem to be trumped by individual variation among students. In other words, there were participants in each group whose emotions (one or more) remained relatively stable from one visit to the next through the SL experience, such as those who exhibited abrupt rises and falls in the case of a specific visit, as well those who went through what could be described as an emotional rollercoaster (cf. Dewaele, 2021). This shows yet again that specific constellations of emotions are an outcome of intricate interactions between ID factors and contextual influences (e.g., type of online environment, activities in which learners engage, interlocutors they meet, etc.), an issue that surely deserves further empirical investigation. It should also be pointed out that the results of the study are by and large in line with those of previous research that has provided clear evidence for temporal changes in ID variables, including emotions, over different time-scales in both traditional (e.g., Elahi Shirvan & Taherian, 2021; Elahi Shirvan & Talebzadeh, 2018; Kruk, 2016b, 2018; Kruk et al., 2021; Liu & Xianming, 2019; Pawlak et al., 2020a) and CALL settings (e.g., Kruk, 2019, 2021b, 2021c; Zawodniak & Kruk, 2018b). Many of these studies have also indicated that group patterns are seldom mirrored in the individual trajectories, one more reason to explore factors affecting these trajectories in greater depth.

RQ4: What is the relationship between and/or among the positive and negative emotions in question and is it subject to temporal variation?

RQ4 can be addressed on the basis of two sets of data: (1) the overall, averaged levels of curiosity, enjoyment, boredom and anxiety that the participants in the three groups self-reported during visits to SL, and (2) the intensity of these emotions experienced by individual students in the course of a particular session. When it comes to the former, the answer was in part provided in the discussion focusing on RQ2 above. More specifically, while the overall levels of curiosity and enjoyment in all the groups were high, those of boredom and anxiety were low, only slightly diverging from the general patterns revealed through the analysis of the participants' responses to the four questionnaires tapping their overall emotional profiles with respect to learning English. Even though curiosity showed slightly higher intensity than enjoyment in all the groups and the levels of boredom exceeded those of anxiety with the exception of Group 3, such differences were mostly minuscule and thus negligible. On the whole, such findings could suggest that, in terms of general patterns, higher levels of positive emotions to some extent reduce the chances of the occurrence of negative emotions. With respect to the latter data set (i.e., self-ratings of the four emotions by individual students during each visit), the picture that emerges is much more complex, with this complexity growing as the students' profiles become more diversified (i.e., from Group 1 to Group 3). While it is true that the overall pattern where the positive emotions were high and the negative emotions can be said to have applied to a greater or lesser extent to most participants, there were those in all three groups for whom it was reversed at least during some of the sessions (e.g., Aurora and David in Group 1, Hazel and Isabella in Group 2 or Gianna in Group 3).

This brings us to another issue, which is temporal variation in the relationships among the positive and negative emotions under investigation. The data certainly attest to the existence of such variation, which may have been very pronounced in some students (e.g., the levels of boredom reached those of curiosity and exceeded those of enjoyment for Emma in Group 1 during Session 4) and less evident in others (e.g., for Ava in Group 2 the distance between positive and negative emotions may have risen and fallen over the sessions but their levels never intersected). This shows yet again that the experience of different academic emotions can hardly be seen as predictable

102 *Research findings*

or easily manipulated through a particular mode of learning, because both learner-internal and learner-external factors are bound to conspire to produce intricate emotional reactions in different situations. Since the relationships regarding this particular constellation of positive and negative emotions have not yet been examined, either at one point in time or over time, situating the findings against the backdrop of existing empirical evidence represents a major challenge. Still, the results correspond to some extent to those of previous studies undertaken in traditional and online settings that have shown, for example, a negative correlation between enjoyment and anxiety, pointing to the fact that these are distinct emotions, but also provide evidence for a positive link between boredom and anxiety (e.g., Dewaele & MacIntyre, 2014; Elahi Shirvan & Taherian, 2021; Kruk, 2019, 2021b). As regards temporal variation in the relationships of the investigated emotions, changes over different timescales in this respect have previously been reported, for example, in the case of boredom, anxiety, motivation, and willingness to communicate (Kruk, 2016a, 2021b; Zawodniak & Kruk, 2018b). Surely, there is a clear need to obtain further insights into how such relationships fluctuate in the case of the four emotions that were investigated in the present study.

RQ5: What factors cause the positive and negative emotions and what influences are responsible for changes in the experience of these emotions?

Before focusing on factors responsible for the occurrence of positive and negative emotions as well as changes in their intensity, several important caveats are in order. First and foremost, the analysis clearly demonstrated that it is not really feasible in most cases to tease apart the emotions of curiosity, enjoyment, boredom and anxiety for the simple reason that they tended to interact with each other, which is in line with the claims of complex dynamic systems theory (CDST) (Larsen-Freeman & Cameron, 2008; Li et al., 2020). For example, a student may have been curious about his or her interlocutor who came from an unknown country (e.g., Japan), but at the same time experienced anxiety about the ability to express his or her feelings and thoughts in English, which, in turn, might have reduced the levels of enjoyment. By the same token, repetitive topics could have induced a degree of boredom, but curiosity was still quite high because of the opportunities to practice the TL. What is more, closely related to the previous point, it was difficult in many cases to unambiguously pin down factors that contributed to one of the four emotions and they were bound to simultaneously affect other emotions as well. Similarly, it was not possible to determine which factors triggered specific emotions and which of them were accountable for subsequent fluctuations in their intensity. These issues should be kept in mind when going over those factors later in this section. Finally, it should also be emphasized that no noteworthy differences were detected between Groups 1, 2 and 3 with respect to the causes of their emotional reactions and changes in such reactions over time, with the result that no attempt is made to separate them based on the identified student profiles.

Research findings 103

When it comes to the feeling of curiosity, it was fueled by the desire to get to know the new environment and try out its exciting functionalities, visit foreign places that are inaccessible in reality, especially in times of the pandemic, talk to people of different nationalities and, quite naturally for this group of participants, to improve TL skills. What we can observe here then is an interesting amalgam of general curiosity, both in terms of the presence of an optimal amount of arousal related to the presence of novelty (Spielberger & Starr, 1994) and the occurrence of both I-type and D-type curiosity (Litman, 2010), as well as L2 curiosity, related not only to opportunities to use the TL for communication and to get to know the L2 system as such (e.g., new words and phrases) (Mahmoodzadeh & Khajavy, 2019). This is without doubt the corollary of the informal nature of the language experience where students could make choices as to what context (e.g., places, experience, etc.) will be talked about through the medium of the TL, a situation that is by definition difficult to achieve in the classroom. Not surprisingly, curiosity had a tendency to diminish when repetitiveness set in or very similar topics were discussed. An increase in the level of enjoyment was for the most part brought about by similar factors as for curiosity, but some additional variables also played a part such as the interlocutor (i.e., familiarity, his or her behavior, but also simply TL proficiency), evolving beliefs about the utility of SL as a learning environment, as well as a sense of accomplishment when the communicative goals were attained without any problems. On the whole, it would seem that in the virtual environment represented by SL where learners can make the choice as to whom they start talking and about what, and choose when to terminate the interaction, it is not only mainly the private but also the social dimension of enjoyment that played a key role (cf. Dewaele & MacIntyre, 2016). Such circumstances are certainly not the norm in most classrooms. Similar to curiosity, it was repetitiveness of topics and situations that led to a decrease in enjoyment, but in this case this positive feeling was also dampened by the difficulty of finding one's way around SL, insufficient experience in employing technology, technical problems, interlocutors' low level of English proficiency or their refusal to speak this language but also, perhaps most importantly, their inappropriate behavior (e.g., sexual innuendos).

Moving on to negative emotions, in line with the previous findings, they were often on the decline when the levels of curiosity and enjoyment were high, but this was by no means always the case. An increase in the level of boredom was typically associated with lack of novelty, repetitiveness or inadequate challenge (e.g., very low level of interlocutors' TL), which can be accounted for in terms of both the under-stimulation model (Larson & Richards, 1991) and the forced-effort model (Hill & Perkins, 1985; Pekrun et al., 2010). Interestingly, though, in line with the dimensional model (Pekrun et al., 2010), there were situations in which prolonged periods of boredom led to an explosion of curiosity, enjoyment and, one could also assume, motivation, once an inspiring SL user was encountered and an interesting interaction in English ensued. When it comes to anxiety, while it often did take the

104 *Research findings*

form of communication apprehension related to the fear of not being sufficiently proficient (Horwitz et al., 1986), it was also caused by factors that were unrelated to L2 learning, which included, for example, the need to move around an unknown environment, lack of adequate computer skills, the unpredictable or unacceptable behavior of interlocutors, as well as the related feelings of insecurity. This shows once again that in the case of informal learning in virtual environments some new dimensions of emotional reactions come into play that are seldom encountered in the classroom. Looking at the qualitative data, one could also get the impression that in some cases anxiety could have been facilitative in nature, particularly in situations when it did appear but its levels were lower than those of the positive emotions of curiosity and enjoyment. On the whole, many of the factors that brought about changes in the emotions under investigation are similar to those identified in previous studies (e.g., Elahi Shirvan & Taherian, 2018; Kruk, 2016a, 2018, 2021a, 2021b; Yoshida, 2020a). A valuable finding of this study, however, is that it showed quite convincingly the impact of social issues, not directly related to language learning, on the interplay of positive and negative emotions. Moreover, it is clear from the analyses that, just as Sampson and Yoshida (2020) showed, similar situations may evoke disparate emotional reactions, which, yet again, can be put down to individual learner profiles or contextual issues, but could also be illustrative of the fact that the students may have followed somewhat different agendas when using SL.

Limitations

While the research project has surely shed some interesting new light on the interactions among positive and negative emotions in virtual environments such as SL, and has helped us somewhat better understand the reasons for the dynamicity of such emotions, the study is not free from a number of limitations. First, as was the case with many previous investigations, the participants were university students majoring in English, which somewhat by default results in a relatively stable initial emotional profile, where the impact of positive emotions surpasses that of negative emotions. Although, as has been shown in this and previous studies, such general patterns do not have to be mirrored for individual students, they will inevitably be transposed into the learning activities in which students engage in the classroom and outside. Second, the analyses did not take into account variables that could have allowed more profound understanding of the occurrence and fluctuations of curiosity, enjoyment, boredom and anxiety, such as some ID factors (e.g., attitudes, beliefs, learning styles, learning strategies, motivation, personality) but also the level of TL proficiency of the participants, whether more objective (e.g., in terms of examination scores) or more subjective (i.e., in terms of some self-evaluation measures). This could have surely made it possible to probe deeper into the causes of individual variation in the experience of the positive and negative emotions, but it could have also allowed reliance on additional dimensions when trying to identify the students' profiles. Third, not only did the number of visits to SL vary for the participants, but there is also very little information about the duration and nature of these sessions. Had there been a possibility of tracking students' actions in real time and making it possible to indicate their emotions at that time, it would have been possible to gain valuable insights into the role of emotions in such informal learning. This, however, would require a different type of study, one that will hopefully be undertaken in the near future. Fourth, the insights obtained could have been enhanced by the inclusion of scales that focused on the four emotions under investigation, specifically with respect to L2 learning in online environments, but such questionnaires have yet to be developed. Fifth, additional insights could have been obtained through interviews with the participants, perhaps focused on the information they provided in the narratives. Such issues should definitely be taken into account when conducting future empirical investigations on emotions in online environments.

Conclusion

The present chapter has presented the findings of the study tapping into the intensity, dynamics and interrelationships of positive and negative emotions in informal learning of English as a foreign language in the virtual environment of SL. Despite some weaknesses, the investigation has certainly considerably extended our understanding of how curiosity, enjoyment, boredom and anxiety interact in such settings and what factors underpin such interactions, not least because this constellation of emotional reactions has not previously been examined. Perhaps the most valuable finding of the study was that general levels of emotions established by means of commonly used questionnaires predicted to a considerable extent the patterns of these emotions as they were self-reported during the visits to SL, even if a fair amount of individual variation was inevitably observed as well. Another interesting insight is related to the role of a variety of social factors in shaping motivational reactions, factors that are often difficult to pinpoint in the classroom because of the nature of L2 instruction in many contexts. This is because informal learning in virtual environments allows a degree of autonomy in what to learn, when and with whom, that traditional classrooms can barely ever afford. Based on these findings, an attempt will be made to offer a handful of pedagogical implications and suggest some future research directions in the conclusion to the volume.

Note

1 It should be noted that major language mistakes found in the excerpts were corrected during the analysis.

Conclusion

The present volume has been dedicated to the empirical investigation of the experience of both positive (i.e., curiosity and enjoyment) and negative (i.e., boredom and anxiety) emotions by advanced L2 learners (i.e., university students majoring in English) in the virtual world SL. Out of the four emotions, second language acquisition (SLA) researchers have given the most attention to the experience of anxiety and enjoyment in L2 learning and teaching in traditional and, in the case of the negative emotion of anxiety, also computer-assisted language learning (CALL) settings. The same cannot be said about the positive emotion of curiosity and the aversive emotion of boredom in learning and teaching foreign/second languages in both conventional and CALL settings, including virtual environments. This is particularly true about the latter context, which to a large extent remains *terra incognita* not only for these two emotions but for the majority of emotions experienced by students while learning an L2.

The research project reported in this monograph was intended to rectify this problem, at least partly, by exploring the emotions of curiosity, enjoyment, boredom and anxiety in the virtual environment of Second Life (SL). The participants were Polish university students majoring in English, who, due to the Covid-19 pandemic, were asked to use the virtual world SL informally, that is, in their own time, which allowed them to make key decisions about when to learn, how and with whom, thereby exercising their autonomy. The data were collected by means of a number of research instruments that were either originally developed by SLA specialists or were modifications of existing research tools employed in prior empirical investigations conducted by the present authors. The reported analyses relied on both quantitative and qualitative analyses. The results shed light on the levels of the four emotions experienced by the participants in their endeavors to learn English in SL, the dynamics of these emotions, the relationships among them, as well as factors that caused them and influences accountable for changes in the intensity of their experience. In view of the fact that the results of the study and their discussion were reported in detail in Chapter 4, a general summary of the findings will only be presented at this point. In addition, an attempt will also be made to suggest a number of pedagogical implications and outline directions for future empirical investigations.

DOI: 10.4324/9781003240068-6

Conclusion 107

The analysis of the data collected by means of the LLCS, LLES, BPELC-R and FLCA scales concerning the experience of the four emotions in conventional contexts revealed that the sample as a whole reported higher levels of positive emotions than the negative ones, which turned out to be experienced at a high or neutral level (cf. Wattana, 2013). In addition, meticulous analysis of the students' responses to the four scales made it possible to identify three distinct profiles of the students who participated in the research project. They included: (1) participants who exhibited very high or high levels of positive emotions versus neutral or low levels of negative emotions, (2) students who demonstrated a very high or high level of one positive emotion and neutral or low levels of negative and positive emotions, and (3) individuals who represented a combination of high/neutral/low levels of positive and/or negative emotions. The patterns of the reported emotions experienced by the participants in learning English as a foreign language in general to a large extent mirrored those that participants indicated in their self-ratings of these emotions experienced during visits to SL. More specifically, on the whole, the learners exhibited higher levels of positive than negative emotions. Interestingly, though, the difference between curiosity and enjoyment shrank, whereas the intensity of negative emotions proved to be lower in this case (cf. Wattana, 2013) when compared to the levels of the negative emotions displayed by the results obtained through the LLCS, LLES, BPELC-R and FLCA scales. In addition, the level of boredom slightly surpassed the level of anxiety.

The analysis of the data provided in the emotional grid included in the in-world session log showed that, generally, the levels of the investigated emotions fluctuated from one session in SL to another; however, periods of stability could also be detected in the data. When it comes to the relationship between and/or among the positive and negative emotions as well as their temporal variation in SL, the findings suggested that, overall, higher levels of positive emotions to some degree diminished the chances of the manifestation of negative emotions in the three groups. Positive emotions were also found to be less susceptible to fluctuations than negative ones. The situation turned out to be more complex in the case of individual students since, as the detailed analysis of the patterns demonstrated, the levels of the emotions under study, both positive and negative, deviated from the general trend. The data also indicated the existence of temporal variation in the relationships among the investigated emotions, although such variation was more detectable in some individual students and less visible in other learners.

As far as factors causing the positive and negative emotions and influences accountable for changes in the experience of these emotions are concerned, it was found that the feeling of curiosity was generated, for example, by the craving to get to know the new virtual environment, visit different locations, communicate with SL users and practice English. As for the experience of enjoyment, it was fueled, among other things, by the participants' interlocutors, students' developing beliefs about the value of SL as an environment for practicing target language skills, feelings of success when goals were

108   *Conclusion*

accomplished without any problems, and factors similar to those concerning the emotion of curiosity. A negative influence on these two positive emotions was brought about by a similar set of factors, which, among others, included repetitiveness, interactions about similar topics, unwillingness to converse in English on the part of some SL residents, their low level of English proficiency, inappropriate behavior of some SL users, as well as some technical problems and insufficient computer skills. As regards factors accountable for an increase in the levels of the negative emotions of boredom and anxiety, in the former case they included, for example, lack of novelty, repetitiveness and inadequate challenge, and in the latter case, they mostly pertained to communication apprehension (Horwitz et al., 1986) and factors unrelated to L2 learning (e.g., lack of satisfactory computer skills, unpredictable behavior of SL users). Although some of the factors responsible for fluctuations in the four emotions were also recognized in earlier studies (e.g., Kruk, 2019, 2021b), the present empirical investigation revealed the influence of social issues on the relationship among positive and negative emotions.

The findings of the research project provide a basis for a number of tentative pedagogical implications that, although mainly intended for learners of English as a foreign language, especially those at higher proficiency levels such as university students majoring in English, may also be applied to learners of other foreign languages in both formal and informal settings. These recommendations are also meant to maximize the intensity of positive emotions and minimize the experience of negative emotions in virtual environments such as SL. First, it would seem necessary to provide language learners with a list of unique locations they could exploit before a visit to a virtual world, which, among other things, would be of interest to language learners, include an element of the unknown or resemble a known location but, for various reasons, constitute an inaccessible place in the real world at a given point in time. Second, it would be advisable to develop language tasks and activities in such a way that they include a social component, that is, tasks that would offer language learners opportunities to communicate with a number of interlocutors representing not only their classmates but also peers from partner educational institutions/schools, either from the country of a learners' origins or from abroad. However, it is of crucial importance that, if invited conversation partners are not native speakers of a target language, they represent an appropriate level of that language, at least such that allows successful communicative interactions. Third, the tasks to be performed by language learners in a virtual world should vary, that is, they should not be repetitive and monotonous. In addition, they should pose a challenge for students but at the same time be attainable for them. Such tasks may be prepared in collaboration with the teacher but also students' peers from different contexts. Fourth, students who are unfamiliar with virtual environments, such as the virtual world SL, or those who do not possess sufficient skills needed for successfully using computer technology, should have the opportunity to benefit from properly designed preparatory sessions in which they would be trained in basic computer skills and instructed in how to effectively use such digital

Conclusion   109

environments for the purpose of L2 learning. Fifth, students should be trained in the use of tools available in a specific virtual world. For example, they should be shown how to interact with virtual objects, how to build virtual objects, make use of and share presentations and, above all, they should be instructed in the use of voice utilities as this might reduce their tendency to mostly rely on text-based messages. Sixth, it would be beneficial for L2 education if virtual worlds constituted an integral part of a physical classroom in the sense that they might be used as an extension of it for either all students or those who would like to practice their TL skills in a more natural environment in their own time. Obviously, it is also possible to extend such opportunities to homework assignments or to simply raise students' awareness of the possibility of using such environments for L2 learning in their own time. Seventh, and most importantly perhaps, students should be constantly reminded of the dangers inherent to online environments and that "safety protocols" (i.e., a list of issues that should be avoided, for example, disclosure of one's real identity and one's sensitive information) should always be observed by each individual who decides to enter a virtual world for the purpose of learning a foreign/second language.

Even though the present investigation has shed new light on the role of emotions in L2 learning in online environments, there is certainly an urgent need for further empirical investigations in this area. In the first place, such research should focus on an even wider palette of emotions experienced by language learners in such environments, as well as diverse combinations of such emotions (e.g., curiosity, pride, hope, love, shame, boredom, etc.). Particularly interesting in this respect could be empirical investigations of how the relationships among such emotions are likely to change over time. It would also be interesting to explore how different constellations of emotions are related to learning specific L2 language skills and/or subsystems as well as language tasks and activities. This, of course, would necessitate the inclusion of different measures of attainment, both those more objective (e.g., course grades and examination results) and subjective (i.e., self-evaluation). Future research could also include larger samples of language learners at different educational levels and of varied levels of foreign/second language proficiency. In addition, future studies could include scales that would focus on a variety of emotions specifically designed with respect to L2 learning in digital environments as well as make use of other research instruments, such as, for example, interviews and diaries. Besides data related to the experience of emotions in digital contexts, it would be worthwhile to collect data concerning other variables such as, for example, learning styles, learning strategies and grit, in order to better understand the emotional make-up individuals exhibit during their language adventures in virtual environments. Finally, future studies could employ a variety of statistical procedures that would enable creating models that would offer insights into the complex networks of emotions and other variables that collectively shape L2 learning in digital environments.

Appendix A

The Background Questionnaire

Please provide the following information by writing your response in the space allotted.

Name:

1 Male ... Female ...
2 Age: ... years old.
3 How long have you been learning English? ...
4 What grade did you receive on the end-of-the-year examination in English? ...
5 How would you self-evaluate your knowledge of English (on a scale from 2 to 5)? ...
6 Do you take part in computer-mediated communication (CMC – i.e., communication through e-mails, instant messaging, blogging, Skype, online chatting, etc.) in English? (underline the correct answer)

   Yes No

7 If you take part in CMC, do you do it: *just for pleasure, social reasons* or do you *intentionally plan to improve your English through CMC*? (underline the correct answer)
8 How would you rate your face-to-face communication skills (i.e., your abilities to share information in English with others and comprehend what others are saying in English)? (underline the correct answer)

   Excellent Very good Good Fair Poor

9 How would you rate your CMC communication skills (i.e., your abilities to share information in English with others and comprehend what others are saying in English through e-mails, instant messaging, blogging, Skype, online chatting, etc.)? (underline the correct answer)

   Excellent Very good Good Fair Poor

Appendix A 111

10 Have you ever heard of a virtual world (e.g., Second Life)? (underline the correct answer)

Yes No

11 Have you ever visited a virtual world (e.g., Second Life)? (underline the correct answer)

Yes No

12 Have you ever used a virtual world (e.g., Second Life) for learning/practicing English? (underline the correct answer)

Yes No

Appendix B

Questionnaires Concerning Positive and Negative Emotions

Name:

Language Learning Curiosity

1 I wonder how well I can speak English in contexts outside the classroom.
2 I always like to learn not only the language rules but also the 'exceptions.'
3 When I have a language question in mind, I cannot rest without knowing the answer.
4 I wonder how well I can speak English when meeting a native English speaker.
5 I always like to learn the cultural differences between English and my native language.
6 I wonder how it would feel to speak and write English as well as my language teacher does.
7 When my language teacher corrects my grammatical mistake, I am just curious to know why it is not correct.
8 If I see or hear an unfamiliar English word, I immediately check my dictionary or ask my teacher.
9 I wonder how it would feel to speak English as fluently as a native speaker does.
10 It keeps me occupied if I cannot express what I know from my native language in English.
11 I always like to know how to use the new words I learn in conversational situations outside the classroom.

Language Learning Enjoyment

1 I am motivated to go to my language class because it is exciting.
2 I enjoy being in my language class.
3 I feel excited about being in my language class listening to the teacher.
4 I am glad that it paid off to go to my language class.

Appendix B 113

5 I do not get bored whilst learning English because I enjoy myself in class.
6 I am a worthy member of my language class.
7 I can laugh off embarrassing mistakes in my language class.
8 In my language class, I feel proud of my accomplishments.

Boredom in Practical English Language Classes - Revised

1 Time always seems to be passing slowly in my language classes.
2 I often find myself at loose ends in a language class.
3 I often have to do meaningless things in my language classes.
4 I always feel entertained in my English language classes.
5 I often have to do repetitive or monotonous things in my language classes.
6 It takes more stimulation to get me going in English classes than most students from my group.
7 I get a kick out of most things I do in a language class.
8 I am seldom excited about my English language classes.
9 I can usually find something interesting to do in my language classes.
10 I often do not feel like doing anything in English classes.
11 It would be very hard for me to find an exciting task in language classes.
12 I would like to have more challenging things to do in my English classes.
13 I feel that I am working below my abilities most of the time in my language classes.
14 I am more interested in other subjects than in practical English classes.
15 If I am not doing something interesting/exciting during English classes, I feel tired and bored.
16 It takes a lot of change and variety to keep me really satisfied during my English classes.
17 It seems that English classes are the same all the time; it is getting boring.
18 It is easy for me to concentrate on the activities in my English language classes.
19 During language classes, I often think about unrelated things.
20 Having to listen to my English language teachers present material bores me tremendously.
21 I actively participate in English classes.
22 Much of the time I just sit around doing nothing in my English language classes.
23 In situations where I have to wait (e.g., for everyone to finish their task), I get very restless.

Foreign Language Classroom Anxiety

1 Even if I am well prepared for my language class, I feel anxious about it.
2 I always feel that the other students speak the foreign language better than I do.

114   *Appendix B*

3   I can feel my heart pounding when I'm going to be called on in a language class.
4   I don't worry about making mistakes in my foreign language class.
5   I feel confident when I speak in my foreign language class.
6   I get nervous and confused when I am speaking in my foreign language class.
7   I start to panic when I have to speak without preparation in my foreign language class.
8   It embarrasses me to volunteer answers in my foreign language class.

Appendix C

The in-World Session Log

Name: Date:

Please describe your feelings related to your last session in Second Life. Please write if you enjoyed learning English during this visit and if you felt curious about learning English there. In addition, please write if you experienced boredom and language anxiety in this session. Please consider the following questions: What did you enjoy the most?, What were you curious about?, Who/What made you bored?, When did you feel bored?, Who/What made you anxious?, When did you feel particularly anxious?, etc. Finally, try to rate the levels of English language enjoyment, curiosity, boredom and anxiety on a scale ranging from 1 (minimum) to 5 (maximum).

116   *Appendix C*

Now rate your levels of English language learning curiosity, enjoyment, bore-dom and anxiety (1=minimum; 5=maximum).

curiosity	enjoyment	boredom	anxiety
1 2 3 4 5	1 2 3 4 5	1 2 3 4 5	1 2 3 4 5

References

Acee, T. W., Kim, H., Kim, H. J., Kim, J., Chu, H. R., Kim, M., … Riekenberg, J. J. (2010). Academic boredom in under- and over-challenging situations. *Contemporary Educational Psychology, 35*(1), 17–27.

Ally, M. (2008). What is wrong with current theorizations of 'boredom'? *Acta Academica, 40*(3), 35–66.

Alpert, R., & Haber, R. N. (1960). Anxiety in academic achievement situations. *Journal of Abnormal and Social Psychology, 61*(2), 207–215.

Arnold, J. (1999). *Affect in language learning.* Cambridge University Press.

Arnold, N. (2007). Reducing foreign language communication apprehension with computer-mediated communication: A preliminary study. *System, 35*(4), 469–486.

Arnone, M. P., & Grabowsky, B. L. (1992). Effects on children's achievement and curiosity of variations in learner control over an interactive video lesson. *Educational Technology Research and Development, 30*, 15–27.

Arnone, M. P., Grabowski, B. L., & Rynd, C. P. (1994). Curiosity as a personality variable influencing learning in a learner controlled lesson with and without advisement. *Educational Technology Research and Development, 42*(1), 5–20. https://doi.org/10.1007/BF02298167.

Ataiefar, F., & Sadighi, F. (2017). Lowering foreign language anxiety through technology: A case of Iranian EFL sophomore students. *English Literature and Language Review, 3*(4), 23–34.

Aydin, S. (2011). Internet anxiety among foreign language learners. *TechTrends, 55*(2), 46–54.

Barcelos, A. (2021). Revolutionary love and peace in the construction of an English teacher's professional identity. In R. Oxford, M. Olivero, & M. Harrison (Eds.), *Peacebuilding in language education* (pp. 96–109). Multilingual Matters. https://doi.org/10.21832/9781788929806-011.

Bashori, M., van Hout, R., Strik. H., & Cucchiarini, C. (2020). Web-based language learning and speaking anxiety. *Computer Assisted Language Learning.* https://doi.org/10.1080/09588221.2020.1770293.

Bench, S. W., & Lench, H. C. (2013). On the function of boredom. *Behavioral Science, 3*(3), 459–472.

Benson, P. (2011). *Teaching and researching autonomy in language learning.* Routledge.

Berryhill, J., Linney, J. A., & Fromewick, J. (2009). The effects of education accountability on teachers: Are policies too stress provoking for their own good? *International Journal of Education Policy and Leadership, 4*(5), 1–14.

118   *References*

Botes, E., Dewaele, J.-M., & Greiff, S. (2020a). The development of a short-form foreign language enjoyment scale. *PsyArXiv.* https://doi.org/10.31234/osf.io/984hb.

Botes, E., Dewaele, J.-M., & Greiff, S. (2020b). The power to improve: Effects of multilingualism and perceived proficiency on enjoyment and anxiety in foreign language learning. *European Journal of Applied Linguistics, 8*(2), 1–28.

Boudreau, C., MacIntyre, P. D., & Dewaele, J.-M. (2018). Enjoyment and anxiety in second language communication: An idiodynamic approach. *Studies in Second Language Learning and Teaching, 1*(8), 149–170. https://doi.org/10.14746/ssllt.2018.8.1.7.

Bown, J., & White, C. (2010). A social and cognitive approach to affect in SLA. *International Review of Applied Linguistics, 48*, 331–353. https://doi.org/10.1515/iral.2010.014.

Bronfenbrenner, U. (1979). *The ecology of human development: Experiments by nature and design.* Harvard University Press.

Brumhead, F., Searle, M., Trowbridge, R., & Williams, B. (1990). Boredom in suburbia. *Youth Studies, 9*(4), 19–34.

Caldwell, L. L., Darling, N., Payne, L. L., & Dowdy, B. (1999). "Why are you bored?" An examination of psychological and social control causes of boredom among adolescents. *Journal of Leisure Research, 31*, 103–121.

Chapman, K. E. (2013). *Boredom in the German foreign language classroom* (Doctoral dissertation, University of Wisconsin-Madison). Retrieved from ProQuest Dissertations Publishing (Publication No. 3566370).

Cohen, A. D., Oxford, R. L., & Chi, J. C. (2002). *Learning style survey.* Retrieved from http://www.mrspsela.com/uploads/2/1/8/7/21879712/learning_style_survey_all_students.pdf.

Cook, T. (2006). *An investigation of shame and anxiety in learning English as a second language* (Doctoral dissertation, University of Southern California). Retrieved from ProQuest Dissertations Publishing (Publication No. 3236494).

Coryell, J. E., & Clark, M. C. (2009). One right way, intercultural participation, and language learning anxiety: A qualitative analysis of adult online heritage and non-heritage language learners. *Foreign Language Annals, 42*(3), 483–504.

Council of Europe. (2001). *Common European framework of reference for languages: Learning, teaching, assessment.* Cambridge University Press.

Csizér, K. (2020). The L2 motivational self system. In M. Lamb, K. Csizér, A. Henry, & S. Ryan (Eds.). (2020). *The Palgrave handbook of motivation for language learning* (pp. 71–93). Palgrave Macmillan.

Csikszentmihalyi, M. (2004). Pleasure vs. enjoyment. *Across the Board, 41*(2), 9.

Daniels, L. M., Tze, M. C., & Goetz, T. (2015). Examining boredom: Different causes for different coping profiles. *Learning and Individual Differences, 37*, 255–261.

Davies, J., & Fortney, M. (2012). *The menton theory of engagement and boredom* (pp. 131–143). Poster presented at the First Annual Conference on Advances in Cognitive Systems, Palo Alto, CA.

Derakhshan, A., Kruk, M., Mehdizadeh, M., & Pawlak, M. (2021). Boredom in online classes in the Iranian EFL context: Sources and solutions. *System, 101*, 102556. https://doi.org/10.1016/j.system.2021.102556.

De Smet, A., Mettewie, L., Galand, B., Hiligsmann, P., & Van Mensel, L. (2018). Classroom anxiety and enjoyment in CLIL and non-CLIL: Does the target language matter? *Studies in Second Language Learning and Teaching, 8*(1), 47–71. https://doi.org/10.14746/ssllt.2018.8.1.3.

References 119

Dewaele, J.-M. (2002). Psychological and sociodemographic correlates of communicative anxiety in L2 and L3 production. *International Journal of Bilingualism, 6*(1), 23–38. https://doi.org/10.1177%2F13670069020060010201.

Dewaele, J.-M. (2005). Investigating the psychological and emotional dimensions in instructed language learning: Obstacles and possibilities. *Modern Language Journal, 89*, 367–380. https://doi.org/10.1111/j.1540-4781.2005.00311.x.

Dewaele, J.-M. (2009). Perception, attitude and motivation. In V. Cook & Li Wei (Eds.), *Language teaching and learning* (pp. 163–192). Continuum.

Dewaele, J.-M. (2011). Reflections on the emotional and psychological aspects of foreign language learning and use. *Anglistik, 22*(1), 23–42.

Dewaele, J.-M. (2021). The emotional rollercoaster ride of foreign language learners and teachers: Sources and interactions of classroom emotions. In M. Simons & T. F. H. Smits (Eds.), *Language education and emotions: Research into emotions and language learners, language teachers and educational processes* (pp. 205–220). Routledge.

Dewaele, J.-M., & Alfawzan, M. (2018). Does the effect of enjoyment outweigh that of anxiety in foreign language performance? *Studies in Second Language Learning and Teaching, 8*(1), 21–25. https://doi.org/10.14746/ssllt.2018.8.1.2.

Dewaele, J.-M., & Dewaele, L. (2017). The dynamic interactions in foreign language classroom anxiety and foreign language enjoyment of pupils aged 12 to 18: A pseudo-longitudinal investigation. *Journal of the European Second Language Association, 1*, 11–22.

Dewaele, J.-M., & Dewaele, L. (2020). Are foreign language learners' enjoyment and anxiety specific to the teacher? An investigation into the dynamics of learners' classroom emotions. *Studies in Second Language Learning and Teaching, 10*(1), 45–65. https://doi.org/10.14746/ssllt.2020.10.1.3.

Dewaele, J.-M., & Li, C. (2020). Emotions in second language acquisition: A critical review and research agenda. *Foreign Language World, 196*(1), 34–49.

Dewaele J. M., & Li, C. (2021). Teacher enthusiasm and students' social-behavioral learning engagement: The mediating role of student enjoyment and boredom in Chinese EFL classes. *Language Teaching Research, 25*(6), 1–24. https://doi.org/10.1177/13621688211014538.

Dewaele, J.-M., & MacIntyre, P. D. (2014). The two faces of Janus? Anxiety and enjoyment in the foreign language classroom. *Studies in Second Language Learning and Teaching, 4*(2), 237–274. https://doi.org/10.14746/ssllt.2014.4.2.5.

Dewaele, J.-M., & MacIntyre, P. D. (2016). Foreign language enjoyment and foreign language classroom anxiety: The right and left feet of the language learner. In P. D. MacIntyre, T. Gregersen, & S. Mercer (Eds.), *Positive psychology in SLA* (pp. 215–236). Multilingual Matters.

Dewaele, J.-M., & MacIntyre, P. D. (2019). The predictive power of multicultural personality traits, learner and teacher variables on foreign language enjoyment and anxiety. In M. Sato & S. Loewen (Eds.), *Evidence-based second language pedagogy: A collection of instructed second language acquisition studies* (pp. 263–286). Routledge.

Dewaele, J.-M., & Pavelescu, L. M. (2021). The relationship between incommensurable emotions and willingness to communicate in English as a foreign language: A multiple case study. *Innovation in Language Learning and Teaching, 15*(1), 66–80. https://doi.org/10.1080/17501229.2019.1675667.

Dewaele, J.-M., & Proietti Ergün, A. L. (2020). How different are the relations between enjoyment, anxiety, attitudes/motivation and course marks in pupils'

120   References

Italian and English as foreign languages? *Journal of the European Second Language Association*, *4*, 45–57.

Dewaele, J.-M., Gkonou, C., & Daubney, M. (Eds.). (2017). *New insights into language anxiety: Theory, research and educational implications*. Multilingual Matters.

Dewaele, J.-M., Özdemir C., Karci, D., Uysal, S., Özdemir, E. D., & Balta, N. (2019). How distinctive is the foreign language enjoyment and foreign language classroom anxiety of Kazakh learners of Turkish? *Applied Linguistics Review*. https://doi.org/10.1515/applirev-2019-0021.

Dewaele, J.-M., Witney, J., Saito, K., & Dewaele, L. (2018). Foreign language enjoyment and anxiety in the FL classroom: The effect of teacher and learner variables. *Language Teaching Research*, *22*(6), 676–697. https://doi.org/10.1177%2F1362168817692161.

Dörnyei, Z. (2007). *Research methods in applied linguistics*. Oxford University Press.

Dörnyei, Z. (2009). The L2 motivational self system. In Z. Dörnyei & E. Ushioda (Eds.), *Motivation, language identity and the L2 self* (pp. 9–42). Multilingual Matters.

Eastwood, J. D., Cavaliere, C., Fahlman, S. A., & Eastwood, A. E. (2007). A desire for desires: Boredom and its relation to alexithymia. *Personality and Individual Differences*, *42*(6), 1035–1045.

Eastwood, J. D., Frischen, A., Fenske, M. J., & Smilek, D. (2012). The unengaged mind: Defining boredom in terms of attention. *Perspectives on Psychological Science*, *7*(5), 482–495.

Elahi Shirvan, M., & Taherian, T. (2018). Anxiety dynamics in a virtual foreign language learning course. *Konin Language Studies*, *6*(4), 411–436.

Elahi Shirvan, M., & Taherian, T. (2021). Longitudinal examination of university students' foreign language enjoyment and foreign language classroom anxiety in the course of general English: Latent growth curve modeling. *International Journal of Bilingual Education and Bilingualism*, *24*(1), 31–49. https://doi.org/10.1080/13670050.2018.1441804.

Elahi Shirvan, M., & Talebzadeh, N. (2018). Exploring the fluctuations of foreign language enjoyment in conversation: An idiodynamic perspective. *Journal of Intercultural Communication Research*, *47*(1), 21–37. https://doi.org/10.1080/17475759.2017.1400458.

Ellis, R. (2008). *The study of second language acquisition*. Oxford University Press.

Eren, A., & Coskun, H. (2016). Students' level of boredom, boredom coping strategies, epistemic curiosity, and graded performance. *Journal of Educational Research*, *109*(6), 574–588. https://doi.org/10.1080/00220671.2014.999364.

Fahlman, S. A. (2009). *Development and validation of the Multidimensional State Boredom Scale* (Doctoral dissertation, York University). Retrieved from ProQuest Dissertations & Theses.

Farmer, R. F., & Sundberg, N. D. (1986). Boredom proneness: The development and correlates of a new scale. *Journal of Personality Assessment*, *50*(1), 4–17.

Feldman Barrett, L. (2017). *How emotions are made: The secret life of the brain*. Houghton Mifflin Harcourt.

Fisherl, C. D. (1993). Boredom at work: A neglected concept. *Human Relations*, *46*(3), 395–417. https://doi.org/10.1177%2F001872679304600305.

Fraschini, N., & Tao, Y. (2021). Emotions in online language learning: Exploratory findings from an *ab initio* Korean course. *Journal of Multilingual and Multicultural Development*. https://doi.org/10.1080/01434632.2021.1968875.

References   121

Fredrickson, B. L. (1998). What good are positive emotions? *Review of General Psychology, 2*(3), 300–319. https://doi.org/10.1037/1089-2680.2.3.300.

Fredrickson, B. L. (2001). The role of positive emotions in positive psychology: The broaden-and-build theory of positive emotions. *American Psychologist, 56*(3), 218–226. https://doi.org/10.1037/0003-066X.56.3.218.

Fredrickson, B. L. (2003). The value of positive emotions: The emerging science of positive psychology looks into why it's good to feel good. *American Scientist, 91*, 330–335. https://doi.org/10.1511/2003.4.330.

Freiermuth, M., & Jarrell, D. (2006). Willingness to communicate: Can online chat help? *International Journal of Applied Linguistics, 16*(2), 189–212.

Frenzel, A. C., Pekrun, R., & Goetz, T. (2007). Girls and mathematics – A "hopeless" issue? A control-value approach to gender differences in emotions towards mathematics. *European Journal of Psychology of Education, 22*, 497–514.

Galmiche, D. (2017). Shame and SLA. *Apples – Journal of Applied Language Studies, 11*, 25–53.

Gardner, R. C. (1985). *Social psychology and second language learning: The role of attitudes and motivation.* Edward Arnold.

Goetz, T., Cronjaeger, H., Frenzel, A. C., Lüdtke, O., & Hall, N. C. (2010). Academic self-concept and emotion relations: Domain specificity and age effects. *Contemporary Educational Psychology, 35*(1), 44–58.

Goetz, T., Frenzel, A. C., Hall, N. C., Nett, U. E., Pekrun, R., & Lipnevich, A. A. (2014). Types of boredom: An experience sampling approach. *Motivation and Emotion, 38*(3), 401–419.

Goleman, D. (2001). An EI-based theory of performance. In D. Goleman & C. Cherniss (Eds.), *The emotionally intelligent workplace: How to select for, measure, and improve emotional intelligence in individuals, groups, and organizations* (pp. 27–44). Jossey-Bass.

Goleman, D. (2006). *Emotional intelligence.* Bantam Books.

Goodwin-Jones, R. (2019). Riding the digital wilds: Learner autonomy and informal language learning. *Language Learning & Technology, 23*, 8–25.

Götz, T., Pekrun, R., Hall, N., & Haag, L. (2006). Academic emotions from a social cognitive perspective: Antecedents and domain specificity of students' affect in the context of Latin instruction. *British Journal of Educational Psychology, 76*, 289–308.

Gregersen, T., MacIntyre, P. D., & Meza, M. D. (2014). The motion of emotion: Idiodynamic case studies of learners' foreign language anxiety. *Modern Language Journal, 98* (2), 574–588. https://doi.org/10.1111/modl.12084.

Grossnickle, E. M. (2016). Disentangling curiosity: Dimensionality, definitions, and distinctions from interest in educational contexts. *Educational Psychology Review, 28*, 23–60. https://doi.org/10.1007/s10648-014-9294-y.

Gruber, J., Mauss, I. B., & Tamir, M. (2011). A dark side of happiness? How, when, and why happiness is not always good. *Perspectives on Psychological Science, 6*, 222–233. https://doi.org/10.1177/1745691611406927.

Harris, M. B. (2000). Correlates and characteristics of boredom proneness and boredom. *Journal of Applied Social Psychology, 30*, 576–598.

Hill, A. B., & Perkins, R. E. (1985). Towards a model of boredom. *British Journal of Psychology, 76*(2), 235–240.

Hiver, P., Al-Hoorie, A. H., & Evans, R. (2021). Complex dynamic systems theory in language learning: A scoping review of 25 years of research. *Studies in Second Language Acquisition.* https://doi.org/10.1017/S0272263121000553.

122 *References*

Hong, J.-C., Hwang, M.-Y., Liu, Y.-H., & Tai, K.-H. (2020). Effects of gamifying questions on English grammar learning mediated by epistemic curiosity and language anxiety. *Computer Assisted Language Learning.* https://doi.org/10.1080/09588221.2020.1803361.

Horwitz, E. K., Horwitz, M. B., & Cope, J. (1986). Foreign language classroom anxiety. *Modern Language Journal, 70*(2), 125–132.

Imai, Y. (2010). Emotions in SLA: New insights from collaborative learning for an EFL classroom. *Modern Language Journal, 94*(2), 278–292. https://doi.org/10.1111/j.1540-4781.2010.01021.x.

Iran-Nejad, A., & Cecil, C. (1992). Interest and learning: A biofunctional perspective. In K. A. Renninger, S. Hidi, & A. Krapp (Eds.), *The role of interest in learning and development* (pp. 297–332). Lawrence Erlbaum.

Jiang, Y., & Dewaele, J.-M. (2019). How unique is the foreign language classroom enjoyment and anxiety of Chinese EFL learners? *System, 82*, 13–25. https://doi.org/10.1016/j.system.2019.02.017.

Jin, Y., & Dewaele, J.-M. (2018). The effect of positive orientation and perceived social support on foreign language classroom anxiety. *System, 74*, 149–157.

Jin, J., Dewaele, J.-M., & MacIntyre, P. D. (2021). Reducing anxiety in the foreign language classroom: A positive psychology approach, *System, 101*, 102604. https://doi.org/10.1016/j.system.2021.102604.

Jin, Y., & Zhang L. J. (2021). The dimensions of foreign language classroom enjoyment and their effect on foreign language achievement. *International Journal of Bilingual Education and Bilingualism, 24*(7), 948–962. https://doi.org/10.1080/13670050.2018.1526253.

Kang, M. J., Hsu, M., Krajbich, I. M., Loewenstein, G., McClure, S. M., Wang, J. T. Y., & Camerer, C. F. (2009). The wick in the candle of learning: Epistemic curiosity activates reward circuitry and enhances memory. *Psychological Science, 20*(8), 963–973. https://doi.org/10.1111/j.1467-9280.2009.02402.x.

Kartal, G., & Balçıkanlı, C. (2019). The effects of Second Life on the motivation of EFL student teachers. In M. Kruk (Ed.), *Assessing the effectiveness of virtual technologies in foreign and second language instruction* (pp. 86–114). IGI Global.

Kasbi, S., & Elahi Shirvan, M. (2017). Ecological understanding of foreign language speaking anxiety: Emerging patterns and dynamic systems. *Asian-Pacific Journal of Second and Foreign Language Education, 2*(1), 2–20.

Kashdan, T. B., Gallagher, M. W., Silvia, P. J., Winterstein, B. P., Breen, W. E., Terhar, D., & Steger, M. F. (2009). The curiosity and exploration inventory – II: Development, factor structure, and psychometrics. *Journal of Research in Personality, 43*, 987–998. https://doi.org/10.1016/j.jrp.2009.04.011.

Kashdan, T. B., Rose, P., & Fincham, F. D. (2004). Curiosity and exploration: Facilitating positive subjective experiences and personal growth opportunities. *Journal of Personality Assessment, 82*(3), 291–305.

Kissau, S., McCullough, H. & Pyke, G. J. (2010). Leveling the playing field: The effects of online second language instruction on student willingness to communicate in French. *CALICO Journal, 27*(2), 277–297.

Kleinginna, P. R., & Kleinginna, A. M. (1981). A categorized list of emotion definitions, with suggestions for a consensual definition. *Motivation and Emotion, 5*(4), 345–379.

Kruk, M. (2016a). Variations in motivation, anxiety and boredom in learning English in Second Life. *The EUROCALL Review, 23*, 25–39.

References 123

Kruk, M. (2016b). Investigating the changing nature of boredom in the English language classroom: Results of a study. In A. Dłutek & D. Pietrzak (Eds.), *Nowy wymiar filologii* (pp. 252–263). Wydawnictwo Naukowe Państwowej Wyższej Szkoły Zawodowej w Płocku.

Kruk, M. (2016c). The impact of using Internet resources and browser-based virtual worlds on the level of foreign language anxiety. In M. Marczak & J. Krajka (Eds.), *CALL for openness* (Vol. *2*, pp. 103–121). Peter Lang.

Kruk, M. (2018). Changes in foreign language anxiety: A classroom perspective. *International Journal of Applied Linguistics, 28*(1), 31–57. https://doi.org/10.1111/ija l.12182.

Kruk, M. (2019). Dynamicity of perceived willingness to communicate, motivation, boredom and anxiety in Second Life: The case of two advanced learners of English. *Computer Assisted Language Learning.* https://doi.org/10.1080/09588221.2019. 1677722.

Kruk, M. (2021a). Variation in experiencing boredom during self-directed learning in a virtual world: The case of one English major. *Australian Review of Applied Linguistics. 44*(3), 289–308. https://doi.org/10.1075/aral.19050.kru.

Kruk, M. (2021b). *Investigating dynamic relationships among individual difference variables in learning English as a foreign language in a virtual world.* Springer.

Kruk, M. (2021c). Fluctuations in self-perceived foreign language anxiety during visits to Second Life: A case study. *Innovation in Language Learning and Teaching, 15*(5), 393–405. https://doi.org/10.1080/17501229.2020.1813737.

Kruk, M., & Zawodniak, J. (2017). Nuda a praktyczna nauka języka angielskiego. *Neofilolog, 49*(1), 115–131.

Kruk, M., & Zawodniak, J. (2018). Boredom in practical English language classes: Insights from interview data. In L. Szymański, J. Zawodniak, A. Łobodziec, & M. Smoluk (Eds.), *Interdisciplinary views on the English language, literature and culture* (pp. 177–191). Uniwersytet Zielonogórski.

Kruk, M., & Zawodniak, J. (2020). A comparative study of the experience of boredom in the L2 and L3 classroom. *English Teaching & Learning, 44*, 417–437. https://doi. org/10.1007/s42321-020-00056-0.

Kruk, M., Pawlak, M., & Zawodniak, J. (2021). Another look at boredom in language instruction: The role of the predictable and the unexpected. *Studies in Second Language Learning and Teaching, 11*(1), 15–40. http://dx.doi.org/10.14746/ssllt.2021.11.1.2.

Lai, C., Zhu, W., & Gong, G. (2015). Understanding the quality of out-of-class English learning. *TESOL Quarterly, 49*(2), 278–308. https://doi.org/10.1002/tesq.171.

Larsen-Freeman, D. (2016). Classroom-oriented research from a complex systems perspective. *Studies in Second Language Learning and Teaching, 6*, 377–393. https:// doi.org/10.14746/ssllt.2016.6.3.2.

Larsen-Freeman, D., & Cameron, L. (2008). *Complex systems and applied linguistics.* Oxford University Press.

Larson, R. W., & Richards, M. H. (1991). Boredom in the middle school years: Blaming schools versus blaming students. *American Journal of Education, 99*(4), 418–433.

Lau, J. K. L., Ozono, H., Kuratomi, K., Komiya, A., & Murayama, K. (2018). Hunger for knowledge: How the irresistible lure of curiosity is generated in the brain. *bioRxiv*, 473975.

Lauriola, M., Litman, J. A., Mussel, P., De Santis, R., Crowson, H. M., & Hoffman, R. R. (2015). Epistemic curiosity and self-regulation. *Personality and Individual Differences, 83*, 202–207. https://doi.org/10.1016/j.paid.2015.04.017.

124 References

Lee, J. S., & Hsieh, J. C. (2019). Affective variables and willingness to communicate of EFL learners in in-class, out of-class, and digital contexts. *System, 82*, 63–73. https://doi.org/10.1016/j.system.2019.03.002.

Lee, J. S., & Lee, K. (2021). The role of informal digital learning of English and L2 motivational self system in foreign language enjoyment. *British Journal of Educational Technology, 52*(1), 358–373. https://doi.org/10.1111/bjet.12955.

LePera, N. (2011). Relationships between boredom proneness, mindfulness, anxiety, depression and substance use. *New Psychology Bulletin, 8*(2), 15–25.

Li, C. (2021). A control-value theory approach to boredom in English class among university students in China. *Modern Language Journal, 105*, 317–334. https://doi.org/10.1111/modl.12693.

Li, C., & Dewaele, J.-M. (2020). The predictive effects of trait emotional intelligence and online learning achievement perceptions on foreign language class boredom among Chinese university students. *Foreign Languages and Their Teaching, 5*, 33–44.

Li, C., Dewaele, J.-M., & Hu, Y. (2021). Foreign language learning boredom: Conceptualization and measurement. *Applied Linguistics Review*. https://doi.org/10.1515/applirev-2020-0124.

Li, C., Dewaele, J.-M., & Jiang, G. (2020). The complex relationship between classroom emotions and EFL achievement in China. *Applied Linguistics Review, 11*(3), 485–510. https://doi.org/10.1515/applirev-2018-0043.

Li, C., Huang, J., & Li, B. (2021). The predictive effects of classroom environment and trait emotional intelligence on foreign language enjoyment and anxiety. *System, 96*, 102393. https://doi.org/10.1016/j.system.2020.102393.

Li, C., Jiang, G., & Dewaele, J.-M. (2018). Understanding Chinese high school students' foreign language enjoyment: Validation of the Chinese version of the Foreign Language Enjoyment Scale. *System, 76*, 183–196. https://doi.org/10.1016/j.system.2018.06.004.

Litman, J. A. (2005). Curiosity and the pleasures of learning: Wanting and liking new information. *Cognition & Emotion, 19*(6), 793–814.

Litman, J. A. (2008). Interest and deprivation dimensions of epistemic curiosity. *Personality and Individual Differences, 44*, 1585–1595. https://doi.org/10.1016/j.paid.2008.01.014.

Litman, J. A. (2010). Relationships between measures of I- and D-type curiosity, ambiguity tolerance, and need for closure: An initial test of the wanting-liking model of information seeking. *Personality and Individual Differences, 48*, 397–410. https://doi.org/10.1016/j.paid.2009.11.005.

Litman, J. A., & Jimerson, T. L. (2004). The measurement of curiosity as a feeling of deprivation. *Journal of Personality Assessment, 82*(2), 147–157. https://doi.org/10.1207/s15327752jpa8202_3.

Litman, J. A., & Pezzo, M. V. (2007). Dimensionality of interpersonal curiosity. *Personality and Individual Differences, 43*(6), 1448–1459. https://doi.org/10.1016/j.paid.2007.04.021.

Litman, J. A., & Silvia, P. J. (2006). The latent structure of trait curiosity: Evidence for interest and deprivation curiosity dimensions. *Journal of Personality Assessment, 86*(3), 318–328. https://doi.org/10.1207/s15327752jpa8603_07.

Litman, J. A., Crowson, H. M., & Kolinski, K. (2010). Validity of the interest- and deprivation-type epistemic curiosity distinction in non-students. *Personality and Individual Differences, 49*, 531–536. https://doi.org/10.1016/j.paid.2010.05.021.

Litman, J. A., Robinson, O. C., & Demetre, J. D. (2017). Intrapersonal curiosity: Inquisitiveness about the inner self. *Self and Identity, 16*(2), 231–250. https://doi.org/10.1080/15298868.2016.1255250.

References 125

Litman, J. A., & Spielberger, C. D. (2003). Measuring epistemic curiosity and its diversive and specific components. *Journal of Personality Assessment, 80*(1), 75–86. https://doi.org/10.1207/s15327752jpa8001_16.

Liu, M. (2009). *Reticence and anxiety in oral English lessons.* Peter Lang.

Liu, M., & Xiangming, L. (2019). Changes in and effects of anxiety on English test performance in Chinese postgraduate EFL classrooms. *Education Research International, 11*, 1–11. https://doi.org/10.1155/2019/7213925.

Loewenstein, G. (1994). The psychology of curiosity: A review and reinterpretation. *Psychological Bulletin, 116*(1), 75–98. https://doi.org/10.1037/0033-2909.116.1.75.

MacIntyre, P. D. (1995). How does anxiety affect second language learning? A reply to Sparks and Ganschow. *Modern Language Journal, 79*(1), 90–99.

MacIntyre, P. D. (2017). An overview of language anxiety research and trends in its development. In C. Gkonou, M. Daubney, & J.-M. Dewaele (Eds.), *New insights into language anxiety: Theory, research and educational implications* (pp. 11–30). Multilingual Matters.

MacIntyre, P. D., & Gardner, R. C. (1989). Anxiety and second language learning: Towards a theoretical clarification. *Language Learning, 39*, 251–275.

MacIntyre, P. D., & Gardner, R. C. (1991). Methods and results in the study of anxiety and language learning: A review of the literature. *Language Learning, 41*(1), 85–117.

MacIntyre, P. D., & Gardner, R. C. (1994). The subtle effects of language anxiety on cognitive processing in the second language. *Language Learning, 44*(2), 283–305.

MacIntyre, P. D., & Gregersen, T. (2012). Emotions that facilitate language learning: The positive-broadening power of the imagination. *Studies in Second Language Learning and Teaching, 2*(2), 193–213. https://doi.org/10.14746/ssllt.2012.2.2.4.

MacIntyre, P. D., & Legatto, J. J. (2011). A dynamic system approach to willingness to communicate: Developing an idiodynamic method to capture rapidly changing affect. *Applied Linguistics, 32*, 149–171. https://doi.org/10.1093/applin/amq037.

MacIntyre, P. D., & Mercer, S. (2014). Introducing positive psychology to SLA. *Studies in Second Language Learning and Teaching, 4*(2), 153–172. https://doi.org/10.14746/ssllt.2014.4.2.2.

MacIntyre, P. D., Noels, K. A., & Clément, R. (1997). Biases in self-ratings of second language proficiency: The role of language anxiety. *Language Learning, 47*(2), 265–287.

Macklem, G. L. (2015). *Boredom in the classroom: Addressing student motivation, self-regulation, and engagement in learning.* Springer.

Mahmoodzadeh, M., & Khajavy, G. H. (2019). Towards conceptualizing language learning curiosity in SLA: An empirical study. *Journal of Psycholinguistic Research, 48*, 333–351. https://doi.org/10.1007/s10936-018-9606-3.

Marsh, H. W. (1992). *Self Description Questionnaire (SDQ) II: A theoretical and empirical basis for the measurement of multiple dimensions of adolescent self-concept: An interim test manual and a research monograph.* Western Sydney University.

McEwan, E. K. (2002). *Ten traits of highly effective teachers: How to hire, coach and mentor successful teachers.* Corwin Press.

Melchor-Couto, S. (2017). Foreign language anxiety levels in Second Life oral interaction. *ReCALL, 29*(1), 99–119. https://doi.org/10.1017/S0958344016000185.

Mercer, S., & Dörnyei, Z. (2020). *Engaging students in contemporary classrooms.* Cambridge University Press.

Mierzwa, E. (2018). The relationship between foreign language enjoyment and gender among secondary grammar school students. *Journal of Education, Culture, and Society, 1*(2), 117–135.

126 References

Miles, M. B., & Huberman, A. M. (1994). *Qualitative data analysis: An expanded sourcebook*. Sage.

Mystkowska-Wiertelak, A., & Pawlak, M. (2017). *Willingness to communicate in instructed second language acquisition: Combining a macro- and micro-perspective*. Multilingual Matters.

Nakamura, S., Darasawang, P., & Reinders, H. (2020). A classroom-based study on the antecedents of epistemic curiosity in L2 learning. *Research Square*. https://doi.org/10.21203/rs.3.rs-47959/v1.

Nakamura, S., Darasawang, P., & Reinders, H. (2021). The antecedents of boredom in L2 classroom learning. *System, 98*, 102469. https://doi.org/10.1016/j.system.2021.102469.

Nett, U. E., Goetz, T., & Daniels, L. M. (2010). What to do when feeling bored? Students' strategies for coping with boredom. *Learning & Individual Differences, 20* (6), 626–638.

Neu, J. (1998). Boring from within: Endogenous versus reactive boredom. In W. F. Flack & J. D. Laird (Eds.), *Emotions in psychopathology: Theory and research* (pp. 158–170). Oxford University Press.

Noels, K. A., Pon, G., & Clément, R. (1996). Language, identity and adjustment: The role of linguistic self-confidence in the acculturation process. *Journal of Language and Social Psychology, 15*(3), 246–264. https://doi.org/10.1177/0261927X960153003.

Norton, B. (2000). *Identity and language learning: Gender, ethnicity and educational change*. Pearson Education.

Palmer, D. (2018). Positive and negative curiosity experiences among tertiary students. *Global Journal of Education Studies, 4*(1), 90–101. https://doi.org/10.5296/gjes.v4i1.13226.

Patall, E. A. (2013). Constructing motivation through choice, interest, and interestingness. *Journal of Educational Psychology, 105*(2), 522–534.

Pavelescu, L. M., & Petrić, B. (2018). Love and enjoyment in context: Four case studies of adolescent EFL learners. *Studies in Second Language Learning and Teaching, 8*(1), 73–101. https://doi.org/10.14746/ssllt.2018.8.1.4.

Pawlak, M. (2012). The dynamic nature of motivation in language learning: A classroom perspective. *Studies in Second Language Learning and Teaching, 2*(2), 249–278. https://doi.org/10.14746/ssllt.2012.2.2.7.

Pawlak, M., Kruk, M., & Zawodniak, J. (2020a). Investigating individual trajectories in experiencing boredom in the language classroom: The case of 11 Polish students of English. *Language Teaching Research*. https://doi.org/10.1177/132168820914004.

Pawlak, M., Kruk, M., Zawodniak, J., & Pasikowski, S. (2020b). Investigating factors responsible for boredom in English classes: The case of advanced learners. *System, 91*, 102259. https://doi.org/10.1016/j.system.2020.102259.

Pawlak, M., Zawodniak, J., & Kruk, M. (2020c). *Boredom in the foreign language classroom: A micro-perspective*. Springer.

Peixoto, F., Mata, L., Monteiro, V., Sanches, C., & Pekrun, R. (2015). The Achievement Emotions Questionnaire: Validation for pre-adolescent students. *European Journal of Developmental Psychology, 12*(4), 472–481. https://doi.org/10.1080/17405629.2015.1040757.

Pekrun, R. (1992). The impact of emotions on learning and achievement: Towards a theory of cognitive/motivational mediators. *Applied Psychology: An International Review, 41*(4), 359–376. https://doi.org/10.1111/j.1464-0597.1992.tb00712.x.

Pekrun, R. (2006). The control-value theory of achievement emotions: Assumptions, corollaries, and implications for educational research and practice. *Educational Psychology Review, 18*(4), 315–341.

References   127

Pekrun, R., Goetz, T., Daniels, L. M., Stupnisky, R. H., & Perry, R. P. (2010). Boredom in achievement settings: Exploring control-value antecedents and performance outcomes of a neglected emotion. *Journal of Educational Psychology, 102*(3), 531–549.

Pekrun, R., Goetz, T., Frenzel, A. C., Barchfeld, P., & Perry, R. P. (2011). Measuring emotions in students' learning and performance: The Achievement Emotions Questionnaire (AEQ). *Contemporary Educational Psychology, 36*, 36–48.

Petrides, K. V. (2009). Psychometric properties of the Trait Emotional Intelligence Questionnaire (TEIQue). In C. Stough, D. H. Saklofske, & J. D. A. Parker (Eds.), *Assessing emotional intelligence: Theory, research, and applications* (pp. 85–101). Springer.

Piechurska-Kuciel, E. (2011a). The relationship between language anxiety and the development of the speaking skill: Results of a longitudinal study. In M. Pawlak, E. Waniek-Klimczak, & J. Majer (Eds.), *Speaking and instructed foreign language acquisition* (pp. 200–214). Multilingual Matters.

Piechurska-Kuciel, E. (2011b). Willingness to communicate in L2 and self-perceived levels of FL skills in Polish adolescents. In J. Arabski & A. Wojtaszek (Eds.), *Aspects of culture in second language acquisition and foreign language learning* (pp. 235–250). Springer.

Plutchik, R. (1980). *Emotion: A psychoevolutionary synthesis.* Harper and Row.

Reeve, J. (2005). *Understanding motivation and emotions* (5th ed.). John Wiley and Sons.

Resnik, P., & Dewaele, J.-M. (2021). Learner emotions, autonomy and trait emotional intelligence in "in-person" versus emergency remote English foreign language teaching in Europe. *Applied Linguistics Review.* https://doi.org/10.1515/applirev-2020-0096.

Roed, J. (2003). Language learner behaviour in a virtual environment. *Computer Assisted Language Learning, 16*(2–3),155–172.

Ross, A. S., & Rivers, D. J. (2018). Emotional experiences beyond the classroom: Interactions with the social world. *Studies in Second Language Learning and Teaching, 8*(1), 103–126.

Ross, A. S., & Stracke, E. (2016). Learner perceptions and experiences of pride in second language education. *Australian Review of Applied Linguistics, 39*(3), 272–291. https://doi.org/10.1075/aral.39.3.04ros.

Rotgans, J. I., & Schmidt, H. G. (2014). Situational interest and learning: Thirst for knowledge. *Learning and Instruction, 32*, 37–50. https://doi.org/10.1016/j.learninstruc.2014.01.002.

Sampson, R. J., & Yoshida, R. (2020). Emergence of divergent L2 feelings through the co-adapted social context of online chat. *Linguistics and Education, 60*, 100861.

Sampson, R. J., & Yoshida, R. (2021) L2 feelings through interaction in a Japanese-English online chat exchange. *Innovation in Language Learning and Teaching, 15*(2), 131–142. https://doi.org/10.1080/17501229.2019.1710514.

Satar, H. M., & Özdener, N. (2008). The effects of synchronous CMC on speaking proficiency and anxiety: Text versus voice chat. *Modern Language Journal, 92*(4), 595–613.

Scherer, K. R. (2000). Emotions as episodes of subsystems synchronization driven by nonlinear appraisal processes. In M. L. Lewis & I. Granic (Eds.), *Emotion, development, and self-organization* (pp. 70–99). Cambridge University Press.

Schumann, J. H. (1997). *The neurobiology of affect in language.* Blackwell.

Scovel, T. (1978). The effect of affect on foreign language learning: A review of the anxiety research. *Language Learning, 28*(1), 129–142.

Scovel, T. (1991). The effect of affect on foreign language learning: A review of the anxiety research. In E. K. Horwitz & D. J. Young (Eds.), *Language anxiety: From theory and research to classroom implications* (pp. 15–24). Prentice Hall.

128 References

Sharp, J. G., Hemmings, B., Kay, R., Murphy, B., & Elliott, S. (2017). Academic boredom among students in higher education: A mixed-methods exploration of characteristics, contributors and consequences. *Journal of Further and Higher Education, 41*(5), 657–677.

Shin, D. D., & Kim, S. (2019). Homo curious: Curious or interested? *Educational Psychology Review, 31*(4), 853–874. https://doi.org/10.1007/s10648-019-09497-x.

Spielberger, C. D. (1983). *Manual for the state-trait anxiety inventory.* Consulting Psychological Press.

Spielberger, C. D., & Reheiser, E. C. (2009). Assessment of emotions: Anxiety, anger, depression, and curiosity. *Applied Psychology: Health and Well-being, 1*(3), 271–302.

Spielberger, C. D., & Starr, L. M. (1994). Curiosity and exploratory behavior. In H. F. O'NeilJr. & M. Drillings (Eds.), *Motivation theory and research* (pp. 221–243). Lawrence Erlbaum.

Tamir, M., & Bigman, Y. (2014). Why might people want to feel bad? Motives in contrahedonic emotion regulation. In W. G. Parrott (Ed.), *The positive side of negative emotions* (pp. 201–223). Guilford Press.

Teimouri, Y. (2018). Differential roles of shame and guilt in L2 learning. *Modern Language Journal, 102*(4), 632–652. https://doi.org/10.1111/modl.12511.

Teimouri, Y., Plonsky, L., & Tabandeh, F. (2020). L2 grit: Passion and perseverance for second-language learning. *Language Teaching Research.* https://doi.org/10.1177/1362168820921895.

Tulis, M., & Fulmer, S. M. (2013). Students' motivational and emotional experiences and their relationship to persistence during academic challenge in mathematics and reading. *Learning and Individual Differences, 27,* 35–46.

van Tilburg, W. A. P., & Igou, E. R. (2011). On boredom and social identity. *Personality and Social Psychology Bulletin, 37*(12), 1679–1691.

Vogel-Walcutt, J., Fiorella, L., Carper, T., & Schatz, S. (2012). The definition, assessment, and mitigation of state boredom within educational settings: A comprehensive review. *Educational Psychology Review, 24*(1), 89–111.

Wang, Y., Derakhshan, A., & Zhang, L. J. (2021). Researching and practicing positive psychology in second/foreign language learning and teaching: The past, current status and future directions. *Frontiers in Psychology, 12,* 731721. https://doi.org/10.3389/fpsyg.2021.731721.

Wattana, S. (2013). *Talking while playing: The effects of computer games on interaction and willingness to communicate in English* (Doctoral dissertation, University of Canterbury). Retrieved from UC Research Repository. http://dx.doi.org/10.26021/9498.

Weinerman, J., & Kenner, C. (2016). Boredom: That which shall not be named. *Journal of Developmental Education, 40*(1), 18–23.

Woodrow, L. (2006). Anxiety and speaking English as a second language. *RELC Journal, 37*(3), 308–328.

Yazdanmehr, E., Elahi Shirvan, M., & Saghafi, K. (2021). A process tracing study of the dynamic patterns of boredom in an online L3 course of German during COVID-19 pandemic. *Foreign Language Annals.* https://doi.org/10.1111/flan.12548.

Yoshida, R. (2020a). Learners' emotions in foreign language text chats with native speakers. *Computer Assisted Language Learning.* https://doi.org/10.1080/09588221.2020.1818787.

Yoshida, R. (2020b). Emotional scaffolding in text chats between Japanese language learners and native Japanese speakers. *Foreign Language Annals, 53,* 505–526. https://doi.org/10.1111/flan.12477.

References 129

Young, D. J. (1991). Creating a low-anxiety classroom environment: What does language anxiety research suggest? *Modern Language Journal*, *75*(4), 426–437.

Zawodniak, J., & Kruk, M. (2018a). Porównawcze studium doświadczania nudy w nauce języków drugiego i trzeciego. *Applied Linguistics Papers*, *25*(3), 149–163.

Zawodniak, J., & Kruk, M. (2018b). Wpływ świata wirtualnego Second Life na zmiany w poziomie motywacji, lęku językowego i doświadczenia nudy u studentów filologii angielskiej. *Neofilolog*, *50*(1), 65–85. https://doi.org/10.14746/n.2018.50.1.5.

Zawodniak, J., Kruk, M., & Pawlak, M. (2021). Boredom as an aversive emotion experienced by English majors. *RELC Journal*. https://doi.org/10.1177/0033688220973732.

Zhao, L., Lu, Y., Wang, B., & Huang, W. (2011). What makes them happy and curious online? An empirical study on high school students' Internet use from a self-determination theory perspective. *Computers & Education*, *56*(2), 346–356.

Index

anger 3–6, 14
anxiety 1–7, 11, 16–20, 22–5, 28–30,
  32–7, 39–42, 44–6, 48–50, 53, 55, 57,
  61, 63–75, 77–89, 91–108, 113–4
apathetic boredom 13–4, 27
ASR-based 40
attentional theory of boredom proneness 14
attitudes 10–11, 29, 38–9, 98, 104
Automatic Speech Recognition 40
autonomy 4, 11, 14, 46, 99, 105–6,
avatar 56, 79, 82–3, 85–9, 93–5

beliefs 16–7, 99, 103–4, 107
boredom 1–3, 5–7, 11–5, 17–21, 25–8,
  30–50, 53, 55, 57, 61–109, 113–4
boredometer 44
breadth/depth curiosity 7–8

calibrating boredom 13, 27
CDST 22, 102
changes 4, 10, 19, 21–5, 28, 30, 33–6, 40–1,
  43, 46, 49, 69, 70–4, 100–2, 104, 106,
CMC 50–4, 110
*cognitive-motivational model of emotion
  effects* 14
complex dynamic systems theory 22,
  36, 102,
complexity 7, 36, 40, 101
*component theories of emotional
  experiences* 15
confidence 5, 24, 33, 35, 37–8, 42
*control-value theory of achievement
  emotions* 14, 31, 39,
COVID-19 43–6, 88, 94–5, 106
culture 4, 6, 11, 38, 44, 78, 80
curiosity 1–2, 6–9, 11, 18–9, 24–5, 33, 39,
  46–50, 53–5, 57, 61, 63, 65–78, 80–5,
  87–109, 113–4

deprivation-type (D-type) curiosity 7–8
deprivation-type epistemic curiosity 39
digital 1–2, 6, 37, 43, 108–9
digital platforms 6
dimensional model 103
dimensions of FLE 10–1
dynamic 2, 7, 17, 22, 25, 35–7, 40–1,
  100, 102
dynamic subsystem regulation 7
dynamically 7, 17, 34
dynamicity 24, 104
dynamics 2, 22, 37, 47, 105, 107

ecosystem model 22
emergency remote teaching 45
emotion theory 15
emotional intelligence 29–30, 39, 46
endogenous boredom 12
enjoyment 1–11, 15, 17–24, 28–30, 33–4,
  38, 40, 43–50, 53–5, 57, 61, 63, 65–75,
  78, 80, 82–5, 87–91, 93–107, 113–4
ERT 45

face-to-face 39, 43, 49–50, 53–4, 91,
  99, 111
FLE 9–11, 20, 29, 43
FLE-Atmosphere 10
FLE-Private 10
FLE-Social 10
FLE-Teacher 10
fluctuate 13, 23, 102
forced-effort model 14, 103
frustration 4–5, 13, 16, 44

gamification 38–9
grid 23–4, 26, 28, 30, 34, 41–2, 55, 57,
  61, 107
guilt 3, 5, 18

happiness 4, 9, 33
hope 3–5, 18, 54, 109

identity 4–5, 44, 92, 109
idiodynamic method 22–3
indifferent boredom 13, 27
information-gap 7
interest-deprivation (I/D) theory of
curiosity 8
interest-type (I-type) curiosity 8
interest-type epistemic curiosity 39
in-world 53–8, 61, 67, 70, 73, 78, 85, 91

L2 communicative curiosity 9, 96
language achievement 5
language curiosity as a feeling-of-depriva-
tion 8
language curiosity as a feeling-of-interest 8
LCFD 8–9
LCFI 8
learning strategies 99, 104, 109
learning styles 27, 41, 98–9, 104, 109
linguistic curiosity 9, 96

menton theory of engagement and
boredom 15
mentons 15
motivation 5, 13–4, 17, 34–8, 41–2,
102–4,
motometer 22, 36
multidimensionality 11
multilingualism 4, 11, 22
multilinguals 4

online classes 43–4, 46, 78, 95
online course 39, 44
online environment 34, 99, 100, 105, 109
online language activities 34
online learning 43, 45–6, 96, 99, 100
online learning platforms 6
online orientation session 56
online session 36
online settings 47, 49, 57, 102
online text chat 6, 37–8, 44
optimal arousal 7, 96

pandemic 44–6, 49, 95–6, 103, 106
perceptual and epistemic curiosity 7
personality 6, 8, 12–3, 17, 43, 92, 104
positive psychology 1, 4, 6
pride 3, 5, 9–10, 19, 29, 33, 45, 47,
54, 109

private dimension 10
profiles 49, 60, 96, 98, 100–2, 104–5, 107

reactant boredom 13
reactive boredom 12
reflective learning 4

searching boredom 13–4, 27
Second Life 6, 15, 34, 48–9, 51–2, 60,
76–81, 83–8, 92, 94, 107, 111, 113
self-esteem 4–5, 17
session log 34–6, 41, 53–8, 60, 64, 67, 70,
73, 107
shame 4–6, 18
SL 6, 34–6, 40–2, 48–9, 55–60, 63–95,
98–101, 103–8
situation-specific anxiety 16–17
social dimension 10, 32, 99, 103
specific/diversive curiosity 7
stability 24, 100, 107
stable 9, 21–2, 24, 29, 33–4, 36, 48, 71,
73–4, 85, 91, 97, 100, 104,
state anxiety 16
state boredom 12–3
state curiosity 7
stress-free 6
synchronous 45, 56

teleport 56
text chats 6, 37–8
thermometer-shaped 23, 36
timescales 23, 30, 48, 101–02
trait anxiety 16
trait boredom 12–3
trait curiosity 7–8
trajectories 26–8, 36–7, 98, 100–1
trajectory 16, 36

under-stimulation model 14, 103

variation 9, 22, 42, 45, 49–50, 61, 66–7,
70–1, 74, 98–102, 104–5, 107
virtual language course 36
voice 56, 58, 76, 90, 109

web-based 40
websites 40
willingness to communicate 4, 17, 24,
36–7, 41, 102
WTC 37, 42

Yoowalk 34

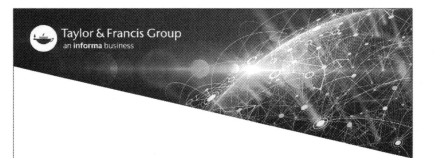